Folk Witchcraft: A Guide to Lore, Land, & the Familiar Spirit for the Solitary Practitioner

ISBN 978-1-7367625-0-9
Moon over the Mountain Press

Folk Witchcraft

A Guide to Lore, Land,
& the Familiar Spirit
for the Solitary Practitioner

Roger J. Horne

Also by Roger J. Horne:

*The Witch's Art of Incantation: Spoken Charms, Spells, &
Curses in Folk Witchcraft*

A Broom at Midnight: 13 Gates of Witchcraft by Spirit Flight

The Witches' Devil: Myth and Lore for Modern Cunning

*Cartomancy in Folk Witchcraft: Playing Cards and Marseille
Tarot in Divination, Magic, & Lore*

Contents

Banishing; Sigils and Incantatory Formulae; Conjuring Spirits; Fetishes and Vessels; Practice: Calling to the Familiar; Practice: The Witch's Altar; Practice: Calling to the Old Ones.

Grammar: Basic Rites
Preface to the Grammar; Tools of the Art; To Lay a Simple Ring; To Lay a More Ornate Ring

Grammar: Sabbat Rites
A Simple Sabbat Rite; A More Ornate Sabbat Rite; The All Hallow's Eve Rite; The Twelfth Night; The Candlemas Rite; The May Eve Rite; The Midsummer Rite; The Lammas Rite; A Simple Esbat Rite; A More Ornate Esbat Rite; A Rite of Dedication

Grammar: Conjurations
Conjuration of Nicneven; Conjuration of the King of Elphame; Conjuration of Aradia; Conjuration of the Folletino Rosso; Conjuration of the Wag at the Wa'; Conjuration of the Hobbitrot; Conjuration of the Black Book of the Art;

Grammar: Various Charms
A Song of Flight to the Sabbat; Another Song of Sabbat-flight; Songs for Going forth as Beasts; The White Paternoster; The Black Paternoster; The Green Paternoster; A Charm for Removal; The Poppet; The Nine Herbs Charm; To Bless or

Curse by Gesture; The Charmed Sachet; Charm of the Firefly; A Counter-charm; To Drive Malicious Spirits from the Home; The Curse of the Evil Eye; To Speak with the Dead; A Braided Charm; To Protect against Maleficium and Evil Spirits; The Witches' Ladder; Talismans; A Lustration Charm; Rowan and Red Thread; A Charm for Prosperity; An Abjuration of the Spirit; Notes on Herbs; Notes on Colors; Notes on Magical Timing; Notes on Cartomancy; Notes on Alphabets; A Witches' Rann.

Preface to the Second Edition

Years ago, when I began drafting the entries and outlines that would become *Folk Witchcraft*, I had little understanding of the ways this work would shape my life and connect me to the lives of others. Having spent a great deal of time trying and failing to fit my practice into the molds of existing modern traditions, and having established an approach to building upon historical charms in my craft, I simply wanted to write the kind of book that I needed in my younger years, the kind of book that would have saved me time and brought me into my own craft faster. I did not expect the book to be loved by readers, but I did hope that it might find the *right* reader, perhaps even one or two young witches somewhere out in the world who were waiting for exactly what a guide like this one would have to offer. The *right* reader. Dozens perhaps. Certainly not hundreds. Definitely not thousands. Although the relative success of *Folk Witchcraft* has been small in comparison to offerings from larger publishers and well-known names, it has been more than I imagined likely or possible.

One of the most frequent comments I receive from readers has to do with how "welcomed" they feel by this book, as if coming home to an old friend or remembering something dear from childhood that they had nearly forgotten. It will not surprise many readers to hear that books have their own spirits, their own guides tucked away within and behind paper, glue, and ink. The spirit guiding my hand in the composition of *Folk Witchcraft* was by my discernment a teaching spirit of a very congenial nature. This guide had a special interest in opening channels of ongoing self-initiation for young witches in the world and reinforcing an ethical framework for collaboration with spirits that did not rest on the constructs of human superiority, violence, and coercion. These two things, in my limited and imperfect opinion, did eventually come to be the two strongest elements at work in the book, and in fact, they are the two things I am most proud of in it.

A question that comes up frequently in my correspondence with readers is the choice of the phrase "folk witchcraft" rather than "folkloric witchcraft" or simply "folk magic." My answer usually comes as a bit of a surprise. In my experience, *folkloric* practice allows us to derive modern rituals from the witch-lore of the past, while *folk magic* represents survived charms and incantations. In folkloric practice, we are reviving the cosmology of forgotten times by transforming lore into ritual; in folk magical practice, we are continuing the legacy of superstitions and day-to-day charms handed down to us. Folk witchcraft, then, is *both*. To describe it as purely folkloric would be like saying that it is entirely lore-born and not culturally alive and vital. To describe it as purely folk-magical would indicate that it is made up of living charms and spells, but has no overarching cosmology or narrative, which is also untrue. *Folk witchcraft* as a term describes the entirety of my practice and the practice of thousands of folk witches around the world, and I am so delighted to have been able to shine a small light upon this spiritual practice that has enriched my life.

Still, despite my overwhelming gratitude for being led into this project, there are things I would have changed or approached differently. This is inevitable in all forms of writing, but especially true in spiritual writing, where text is finite and closed while understanding and feeling continue to grow and evolve over time. I wish I had offered additional notes for complex ideas that merit multiple perspectives and expanded explanations on certain elements of folk craft that can, even at the best of times, feel puzzling. These became my goals for the second edition—in addition to some general but significant updates to formatting.

In many ways, though, there is only so much that can be said about any form of witchcraft without simply diving in, and so I have inevitably failed at capturing the needs of every reader or representing every element of folk craft. I hope the writer's weakness can be forgiven so that the book's initiating spirit may shine through, and really, it is to that spirit that I would ultimately direct the reader anyway—to those threads of initiation that I still believe shape our craft in the most significant ways: lore, land, and the familiar spirit. Getting our hands dirty is always the best way to learn. A book may open the door, but potential, after all, is only polished to perfection by spit and by grit.

Introduction

Let's imagine that we aren't miles apart. We're sitting by a fire, looking out into the mysterious night. It's All Hallow's Eve, so there's a chill in the wind, and the branches of the trees are bare. The stars are bright. Embers from the fire catch on the wind in bright flurries, drifting up into the yawning dark like fireflies. We are here to talk about witchcraft, about spirits, about the land. We are going to talk about the cycles of nature and what they mean. We'll talk about our dreams and visions. We'll nourish our spirits with wisdom from the old lore. Beyond the crackling fire's glow, the shadows lingering between the trees could almost be our ancestors.

In many ways, we are living in the golden age of witchcraft. New traditions are springing up all around us. Writers, bloggers, and vloggers share their approaches and ideas. Scholars have begun to unpack the old lore through the lens of legitimate spiritual experience. Books on the craft are published every day. These modern grammars usually share the author's rituals, their charms, their holidays, and provide a step-by-step approach to conducting craft workings. They try to explain what witches do, what they believe, how they conduct their rituals, what rules they should follow. Sometimes they offer a spurious account of witch history and lineage that leaves the reader more puzzled than before. These books provide much of the *how*, but little of the *why*. Pre-made models and rituals that are practiced without an understanding of their source are like cut flowers: they are beautiful on the kitchen table, but quickly wither away.

This is not that kind of book. Make no mistake; by the end of this book, you will have a treasury of charms, rituals, incantations, and practical methods by which you can conduct your craft. My larger goal, however, is to provide students of the craft with the means by which to connect with the source of witchcraft, those gates of initiation through which any witch worth his salt must pass. Because folk witchcraft is a living tradition, most of us hone and polish our craft over time. We research, experiment, and adapt. We follow the guidance of our familiar spirits. We listen to the land.

The ability to access the currents of magical knowledge at work around us, to hear "the voice of the wind," as the lore says, is central to witchcraft as a living tradition, and in folk witchcraft as a solitary art, anything less simply will not do. The purpose of this book is not to provide the student with merely one approach, but rather, to connect the student to an endless source of continuous learning through the avenues of lore, land, and spirit, to the living roots of witchcraft-as-folk-tradition.

Let's pause for a moment to unpack the phrase "folk witchcraft." I offer this term as a way to distinguish the manner of approach described in this book and as a way to emphasize the role of older lore over witchcraft customs and traditions founded after the popular witchcraft boom of the fifties and sixties. Wicca is the most prominent of these traditions. Folk witchcraft, as I define it here, properly falls within the practices and beliefs popularly referred to as "Traditional Craft," but I cannot help but feel that the word "traditional" implies a cohesive, organized, survived practice, which is inherently misleading since all modern witchcraft entails some degree of reconstruction. Folk witchcraft provides the framework for independent exploration and development in the craft as recorded in our old lore without the shackles of laws and conventions imposed by a modern group's perspective.

Folk witchcraft, then, is both old and new; it is a branch of modern craft firmly rooted in the folklore of witches before the 20th century. The beliefs, rituals, sacred times, and charms of the folk witch are those preserved in the lore, rooted in the land, and won through personal revelations via the familiar spirit. The witch who feels called to the lore may or may possess a genetic lineage to the ancestors of that current, and belonging to a particular ancestral stream by blood does not guarantee success. It is only through the work of witchcraft that these mysteries are won: observing the sacred times with ritual, practicing the charms, conversing with the spirits, and yes, researching your land and your lore. The use of craft sourced in older texts does, in a way, make folk witchcraft different from many contemporary forms of the craft, but not universally so. I tend to think witches have more commonalities than differences, by and large. Thus, the methods and models discussed in this book are intended to be useful to *all witches*.

In order to deliver a practical approach to the old craft, this book will use, as its central metaphor, the clew of Nicneven. A "clew" is an old word for a ball of thread or string, and Nicneven is the name of the Queen and Mother of Witches in Scotland. "Casting a clew" is a reference to an old rite of witchcraft. (I am particularly drawn to Scottish witch-lore.) For our purposes, the three strands of initiation into folk witchcraft are lore, land, and spirit. By drawing from these strands, we can arrive at innovative rituals, creative charms, and personalized practices that are firmly grounded in tradition. Each strand's offerings proceed from the one before it. By learning lore, we identify nature and spirit as consistent sources of power and mystery. By observing the land, we learn the secret to communication and alignment with the familiar spirit, the witch's most perfect guide along the path.

At the end of this book, I offer you a portion of my own grammar of the art and the charms and rituals I've adapted from our lore under the guidance of my familiars. Use them. Change them. Search out the lore from which they spring. Let your own familiars guide you in their use. Let your craft be like a tree, firmly rooted in the old, but stretching into the new. Get your hands dirty, and find out what works and doesn't work for you. As Andrew Chumbley famously wrote, "If you call upon the Gods and they answer, who is there to oppose or to challenge the integrity of your Path?"

Lore

Approaching the Lore

Witchcraft is an old art, and witches love feeling connected to something antiquated and vast, something ancient. Since the modern witchcraft boom of the last century, many writers have put forward claims to authenticity in their lore and traditions, often disputed by scholars. The question of historicity need not be a headache, though. In fact, for the folk witch, connection to the past is everywhere. Folk witchcraft is something we *do*, and it is sourced in our survived lore and charms. The folk witch does not claim to belong to an ancient cultus or an organized religion, but identifies as the inheritor of the specific trappings of our art: the stories, spirits, charms, talismans, incantations, herbs, holy days, and legends handed down to us through the ages.

Disillusioned by a lack of organized authority in modern witchcraft, many students overlook the wisdom in the lore that *has* survived for our benefit. In looking for the password to allow us entry into an ancient priesthood of witches, we are asking the wrong questions, it seems. Rather than seeking a source of singular truth and authority in the craft, we should be asking what secrets the old witch-lore contains and how it can inform our practice. Here are some vital questions:

- *What did people in earlier times believe about witches?*
- *Who were the patron spirits and deities associated with witches?*
- *In what sort of spiritual world did folkloric witches operate?*
- *What sorts of things did the witches of folklore do?*
- *What days and times were deemed especially significant to witches?*
- *What methods of initiation and learning did witches employ?*

Following any of the above lines of inquiry, with the aid of a good library, yields surprisingly rich results. As it turns out, people from earlier times preserved a great deal of information about witches. We must accept, though, that witch-lore is diverse and divergent, that local traditions differ considerably, centering around a few ubiquitous themes:

- *Witches gather in spirit form to feast and celebrate.*
- *Witches perform simple folk magics, usually of the sympathetic and contagious variety.*
- *Witches are able to leave their bodies to fly in spirit or animal spirit form.*
- *Witches are able to travel beneath the land to commune with land spirits.*
- *Witches are instructed in their art by teaching spirits.*
- *Witches are to observe special times related to the seasons.*
- *Witches are connected to the spirits of the dead, the ancestors, and the natural world.*
- *Witches seem to be presided over at their gatherings by authority figures, usually a king and a queen, sometimes one or the other.*
- *Witches blend their art with the trappings of dominant religion.*

The following sections will address aspects of these themes by looking closely at a few particular sources of folklore surrounding witches.

Reginald Scot's *The Discoverie of Witchcraft*, 1584

As a primary source text for early modern witch-lore, *The Discoverie of Witchcraft* is unparalleled. Its depth of study is astounding, even by today's standards. It's clear that Scot's purpose is to convince the reader that witches cannot possibly do the things people believe them capable of, but in the process of following his thesis, he recounts an avalanche of charms, rituals, beliefs, and magical practices attributed to witches by his contemporaries and the popular lore of his era. At times, Scot differentiates between witchcraft and ritual magic. Other times, he sees them as related traditions. Thus, alongside spoken folk charms to heal a wound, we find sigils for the conjuration of planetary spirits and complex talismans, all in one tremendous volume.

Francesco Maria Guazzo's *Compendium Maleficarum*, 1608

One of the great ironies many witches discover in their research is that, while the old witch hunters wrote manuals with the purpose of finding and killing practitioners of folk magic, they inadvertently preserved a wealth of charms for future generations of witches. This is the case with *Compendium Maleficarum*, which is less infamous than the similarly titled *Malleus Maleficarum*, but more noteworthy among folk witches for its lengthy descriptions of specific charms and incantations believed to be used by witches in this period. Although much of the material included in the compendium is designed to paint practitioners of folk magic as diabolic cannibals in order to justify the witch hunter's calling, these elements are easily distinguished by their simplistic tone and the absence of specific examples noted in other sources.

Alexander Carmichael's *Carmina Gadelica*, 1900

The *Carmina Gadelica* is a lengthy collection of Scottish songs, prayers, and incantations that speak to surviving elements of magic and paganism in a christian era. This volume includes healing charms, warding charms, protective charms, blessing charms, prayers to the moon and sun, and many other fragments of spoken magic. Many of these call upon god, the angels, the virgin Mary, or the saints who displaced previous pagan deities, but others call on the forces of nature or specific plants and animals. Even witches who are uncomfortable with the book's christian elements will find a treasury of appropriate charms.

Folger Shakespeare Library MS. V.b.26 (author unknown), late 16th century

Originally a working grimoire without a proper title, this volume has been titled *The Book of Oberon* and reproduced in a beautiful new edition. The book shows how magical material was transcribed into the grimoires of individual practitioners over time. It includes known material from the *Pseudomonarchia Daemonum* and other famous texts, the sort of material used commonly by cunning craft practitioners during the time. Perhaps the most interesting notes in this magical journal include procedures for conjuring spirits who make or give magical books and methods for perceiving spirits, including anointing one's head with "cannabis juice." These elements emphasize the importance of personal revelation via familiar spirits and suggest a different reading of the strange words and sigils in this and other published grimoires.

Charles Godfrey Leland's *Aradia, or the Gospel of the Witches*, 1899

Few other texts have had the lasting impact *Aradia* has had on modern witchcraft. Leland's book is not really a gospel text of any sort, but an amalgam of folklore that is easily traced to rural Italy. Approach it as a series of folktales that Leland strung together, for this is what it truly is. Aradia is a name closely related to Herodias, and in the text, she is portrayed as the first witch in the world. The book includes a description of the witches' supper, a curious creation story associated with Diana and Lucifer, and a rich variety of charms for practical use. The witchcraft described in Aradia leans strongly toward resistance, vengeance, and the defense of the poor and outcast. Diana, in this lore, adopts the marginalized and teaches them the art of witchcraft. She charges her witches with the task of destroying their oppressors in the aristocracy and the church. This book's themes of feminism and personal empowerment have inspired many forms of modern witchcraft.

Nicolas Culpeper's *Complete Herbal*, 1653

Culpeper practiced a form of herbal medicine, and his approach to herbalism was informed by astrology and the "doctrine of signatures," an approach to understanding the components and properties of a plant by carefully observing its characteristics and behavior. Medically speaking, we know more about the properties of herbs today, but magically speaking, Culpeper's approach can help us to reconnect with the art of discernment when it comes to the properties of plant spirits.

Robert Kirk's *The Secret Commonwealth of Elves, Fauns & Fairies: A Study in Folk-lore & Psychical Research*, 1691

Kirk recounts faerie lore and analyzes its relationship to witchcraft, the dead, and survived charms and incantations. His book reveals very clearly that faeries are connected with the realm of the dead. The animist cosmology he establishes in this work is consistent with the approaches of traditional witches today. The lore here is wonderfully specific, citing individual charms and traditions and contextualizing them within a framework of lore.

The History of the Devil, or The Horned God of the West by R. Lowe Thompson, 1929

This book approaches the figure of the folkloric Devil as shamanic in origin, indicating a long-held tradition of sorcerers and witches forging connections to the land and beasts around us. In Thompson's analysis of folklore, cave paintings, and ritual practices, the Devil becomes a kind of emblemized memory of these magical traditions, as well as the "master" of the craft and ancestor of those who practice it. This book is pivotal in its ability to unpack the densely loaded figure of the Devil. There are many lore-born treasures here for the clever witch.

The Golden Bough by William Frazer, 1890

Frazer synthesizes many old world folktales and magical traditions in order to arrive at the central themes and motifs of old paganism. In doing so, he embarks on a lengthy (and, at times, needlessly circuitous) journey across the lore of western Europe. His discussion of the old celtic fire festivals is particularly useful for those interested in the rites and traditions associated with the witches' sabbats. Frazer also analyzes the nature of magical acts and categorizes them by type, providing an anthropological perspective on these traditions. His syncretist approach to understanding how deities blended and became amalgams in the ancient world has greatly influenced how traditional witches approach and the Old Ones.

The Witch-Cult in Western Europe by Margaret Murray, 1921

Murray analyzed the confessions of people convicted during the witch hunts in order to identify patterns. Ignore her thesis. There was no singular, organized witch-cult. Witchcraft has always been a loose term referring to a wide array of practices. What's more, most of the people tried and executed for witchcraft in the early modern era had nothing to do with magic. This is not to suggest that *none* of them did, which would be very difficult for me to believe given the specific details of some of the charms used and the corroborating stories in some of the trials. Regardless, as a source for lore reflecting the popular beliefs of the time, these stories are useful.

T. F. Thiselton-Dyer's *Mythic & Magical Folklore of Plants*, 1899

In this volume, Thiselton-Dyer provides an excellent overview of the relationships between humans and plants and elucidates the theoretical model for understanding how trees, shrubs, and herbs came to be associated with spiritual entities in the lore. The author uses findings from oral traditions, popular sayings, superstitions, and poetry to describe a variety of spiritual traditions around the world centered around plant spirits and their powers.

Plant Lore, Legends, & Lyrics by Richard Folkard, 1892

Folkard connects plant-lore, fairy-lore, and witch-lore in delightful ways. His discussion of plant spirits and folk tales is peppered with poetry and songs that are very conducive to adaptation for incantations and chants. This volume is well-researched and provides more examples and specific details of magical workings with particular plants than Thiselton-Dyer.

One of the challenges that faces new witches is the realization that witchcraft is not an organized religion, that it has no central text, no chain of authority, no standardized structure of worship. Instead, our tradition is inherited in lore and fable, embedded in the stories and charms we have preserved. Faced with this unwieldy prospect, many witches become disillusioned. They ask, "Did no *real* witches exist before the modern era?" Dear reader, of course they did. There were women who knew the powers associated with plants that grew on their land. There were men who could speak with spirits from under the earth. There were folks who could heal a burn or an angry wound using sympathetic charms. There were augurers who could offer counsel from the spirit world. All of them looked to the lore for these incantations and remedies, as you are doing now. What we call witchcraft is a chest that holds all of these treasures from our past. We who call ourselves witches are living proof that these traditions have survived. Look to the lore, put it to use and consider yourself a part of this story.

Magic in Folk Witchcraft

In reviewing the literature from the previous section, the reader will note a multitude of themes that spring up consistently across sources. Modern folk witches hone their rituals and charms around these themes in order to root them firmly in the past. Let's dissect a few of the most important themes that appear in witch-lore in order to assemble a basic structure for the practice of folk witchcraft for the modern solitary practitioner.

In the lore, witches perform magic to help and to hurt. Although many mid-century writers on witchcraft claimed adherence to a "threefold law" or belief in a simplified form of karma that would return a casting to its sender, the lore tells another story. In our stories, witches use their own personal judgment when deciding how to employ their craft. This suggests that their basic moral stance is unique to the individual. No, good

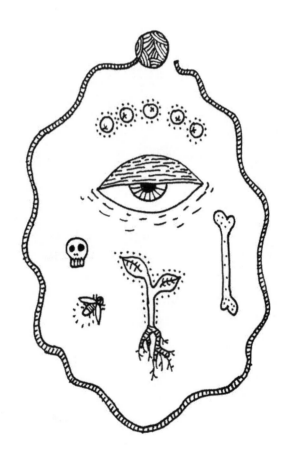

things don't always happen to good people. Those who commit atrocities won't necessarily get their just desserts. If there is to be any justice in this world, it is the justice that we create through our choices and our magics.

The magic performed by witches is frequently either sympathetic or contagious. Sympathetic magic works by using a stand-in for the person who is the target of the magical act. Under this umbrella term fall the use poppets, bread baked in the shape of a person, or acts performed on a graven image. Contagious magic is similar, but works on the principle of proximity: the use of hair or fingernails can bind the charm to the person for whom it is intended. In addition, placing the charm near a person or their property can confer the properties of the charm onto the target. The nature of these workings need not be baneful; charms worked via sympathy and contagion can bring blessings of protection and luck just as easily.

Here, I would like to add a note that is purely personal and anecdotal. Although I don't, as a matter of course, believe in anything like karma, I have observed that magic works through the practitioner, not around him. This means that anything I call forth tends to pass through me on its way out into the world.

Sending a curse, in my experience, is a little like spitting poison from your own mouth. It can be rinsed out, and it isn't a complete return of what you have sent forth, but it changes your spirit ever so slightly. This can mean an amplification of the dark or sinister parts of your personality or the attraction of dark entities, which isn't necessarily a bad thing. It's good practice to be sure the curse is worth it, though, and personally, I don't make a habit of using them.

There are, in numerous sources, specific times identified as propitious for certain types of workings. Curses, hexes (maleficium), and the removal of things is frequently associated with the waning moon. The full moon is associated with powerful magic and is an opportune time for ritual. The waxing moon is a time for positive workings for luck, prosperity, healing, and gain (beneficium). In addition to lunar timings, the days of the week are often identified as useful for determining the timing of a ritual. Sunday is ruled by the sun and is associated with healing, happiness, and good fortune. Monday is ruled by the moon and is associated with the second sight and divination. Tuesday is ruled by Mars and is associated with defense and victory over enemies. Wednesday is ruled by Mercury and is associated with trade, communication, and travel. Thursday is ruled by Jupiter and is associated with prosperity, luck, and favor. Friday is ruled by Venus and is associated with love, friendship, and beauty. Finally, Saturday is ruled by Saturn, associated with curses, the dead, and baneful workings.

In the lore, it is quite common to encounter charms and rituals associated with witchcraft that use christian liturgy, psalms, or Latin prayers for magical purposes. Although many pagans would try to deny it, witchcraft developed into the form we recognize today alongside Christianity, not before it. Our path is not an ancient religion, but a folk tradition incorporating elements of pagan practices alongside adopted bits of Latin incantations derived from church liturgy. In this way, the development of witchcraft is not unlike the development of Voudou or other folk traditions that blend disparate cultural elements. Our ancestors found the Latin language used by christian invaders very strange and mystical, and they sought to use it in their craft, much to the dismay of church authorities. By the early modern period, many old pagan gods had become saints, and identifying as christian was not optional if you wanted to survive. Folks identifying with the cunning craft, the Benandanti tradition, fairy-doctoring, and many other folk practices at the roots of old world witchcraft had fully incorporated christian elements by this time.

From a modern magical perspective, this is very clever, since the working at hand can draw on the egregores of the dominant culture, much like a magical battery. The modern folk witch need not feel any qualms about using psalms and Latin incantations from the christian tradition. This is part of our history. That said, it's perfectly fine to use the names of non-christian entities if one prefers. Accept the paradox of calling on the Devil one minute and reciting a psalm the next. The craft is full of riddles, and there is mystery in the way these elements speak to one another.

The belief in magic is frequently viewed as delusional or superstitious. Bothered by this, some writers attempt to explain the means by which magic operates as a form of primitive psychology, much like repeating an affirmation, wearing piece of jewelry as a reminder of who you want to be, or removing objects and images from your home that remind you of something you wish to be rid of in your life. Personally, I don't think this is inaccurate, per se. I view magic and psychology as two different languages used to describe practices that can overlap, but the language of magic is far older and more fundamental to the human experience than any modern science. The folk witch has no reason or desire to use the language of psychology to explain their craft. We aren't recruiting, so we have no one to convince, and there's nothing to be gained from legitimacy. Folk witchcraft uses the language of magic because magic is the language of our lore.

Spirit Flight in Folk Witchcraft

Even in popular culture, it is generally known that witches fly. What isn't commonly known is that the practice of flight amongst witches was once commonly understood to occur in spirit form, not physical form. In the lore, Scot, Guazzo, and many others attest to this theme. In the *Canon Episcopi*, a medieval church document, the catholic church warned against witches flying by night with Diana or Herodias. The ecstatic experience of leaving one's physical body (the word *ecstatic*, etymologically, referring to being outside oneself) is actually a common spiritual practice in animist cultures around the world.

By traveling in spirit form, magical practitioners in many different cultures are able to interact with spirits, including ancestors, animal spirits, and plant spirits, in order to procure wisdom or cures to bring back to serve the community. In Scottish witch Isobel

Gowdie's confessions, she frequently travels below the hills, which we now know are actually ancient burial sites, in order to dine and converse with the spirits there. Modern folk witches view spirit flight lore as a surviving characteristic from earlier pagan ancestors, and the practice of spirit flight has become one of the defining characteristics of many forms of traditional witchcraft.

Why do we fly? What is to be gained by this excursion into the spirit world and the interactions there? In many ways, the goals of the folk witch are personal and have to do with forging relationships to individual spirits, ancestral streams of power, local wells of energy, but in general, there are certain themes or commonalities that present themselves. The folk witch may fly in order to discern an answer to a complex question requiring one-on-one guidance from a teaching spirit. She may fly in order to visit the target of a charm in spiritual form.

On a symbolic level, our flight practice challenges the empiricism of modern consciousness, specifically the boundaries between dreamed experiences and waking experiences. This is not to suggest that the witch cannot tell the difference between spiritual and physical experience, but that we are redeeming the sacredness of oneiric visionary experiences rather than discarding them as fantasy and rubbish. If we wish our spirits to speak to us, to teach us, to empower us, then we must regard their offered wisdom and interactions as valuable. A regular practice of spirit flight accomplishes this, prioritizing the needs of the spirit alongside the needs of the body and the logical mind.

The Witches' Sabbat

Closely tied to the theme of spirit flight is the folkloric witches' sabbat. When understood through the lens of the previous section, it becomes clear that this gathering of witches and spirits is a spiritual event, not necessarily a purely physical one. Still, witches were observed to conduct their sabbat at specific times, especially on May Eve, All Hallow's Eve, Candlemas, and Lammas. In the old world, May Eve marked the beginning of summer, and All Hallow's Eve marked the beginning of winter. Similarly, Candlemas and Lammas can be said to mark the beginnings of spring and fall, respectively. Since folk practices often entailed offerings to faeries or land spirits on these or similar times, we can say that the sabbat is both a seasonal rite and a spiritual gathering.

The modern folk witches doesn't

strictly adhere to the eight-spoked "wheel of the year" used by other neopagans. We prefer to watch our local landscapes and identify days that correspond to the shifting of the seasons where we live. The wheel of the year is a modern invention, and no pagan societies can be said to have observed all of these dates. It's best to look to the lore for specific rituals for seasonal celebrations. Witches who live in Australia or Iceland may prefer different dates for their seasonal rites. What's important is that the days be governed by the tides of nature, not the shackles of convention.

The symbolic significance of our sabbat is a matter of great discussion and debate, for the themes here are ancient, dating back even to pre-historic cults of spiritual ecstasy that would later evolve into the Bacchanalia. Certain concepts do seem, though, to settle to the bottom of our little pool.

The union of the witch with the spirits of flora and fauna. This principle presents itself in the figure of the devil, who is part human and part goat, as well as in the presence of spirits in the lore who are frequently garbed in green, indicating the green world. On a mundane level, this principle reinforces our interdependence with the natural world and decentralizes human life as neither the most important or most significant, but merely another branch upon the tree.

The union of the witch with the spirits of the dead. The sabbat is frequently held in the lore near graveyards or under "fairy hills," which are actually burial mounds of prehistoric cultures, indicating communion with the dead. On a mundane level, this principle indicates that we are forever connected with our deceased, not separated, and that death and life are but illusions.

The seeking of wisdom and learning from that with frightens us. It is not without meaning that the sabbat of our lore is held at night and in woods, presided over by spirits that appear frightening at first (even if they are actually benevolent to our people). In facing the strange, spiritual other, the witch is slowly freed from the shackles of convention and learns to see beyond initial appearances to appreciate the diversity of our world and the worthiness of all creatures within it.

The prioritization of pleasure and joy over pain and shame. The lore surrounding our sabbat is always somewhat erotic, sometimes detailing sensual encounters between spirits and witches. This process, which can actually be described as a loosening of shame and trauma from our toxic cultures, frequently occurs in spirit flight and is perfectly innocent when conducted respectfully and consensually between both parties.

How individual witches celebrate the sabbat can vary widely. The theme of the feast shared between witches and spirits is common in the lore, and so most witches partake in some form of food and drink, offering a portion to the spirit world. Some conduct spirit flight on these nights in order to experience the spiritual gathering of kindred souls in the otherworld. Most conduct some form of ritual meant to conjure and honor the Old Ones, the ancestors of our craft. These times are deemed especially propitious and potent for magic, and so many important spells and charms are reserved for these dates in order to draw upon that power.

Meetings with Spirits

While many folkloric accounts of witches recount specific charms and remedies that were likely passed down locally, many other witches procured their charms from the direct teachings of spirits. Sometimes these spirits are termed "familiars." Still others take the form of spirits of the dead or great spirits or deities who preside over the activities of witches in the spirit world. Whatever form they take, direct initiation by these spirits, which is an ongoing process of learning and becoming, is pivotal in folk craft.

Many traditional witches will tell you that they were able to perceive spirits from a very early age, which can be disturbing to parents and loved ones. It's important to note that perception of the spirit world is different than regular perception. It isn't the perception of something that is in physical proximity, and it isn't like a hallucination. The fact that these beings exist spiritually and not physically is usually very obvious, and often, witches who are skilled seers can "shut off" their sight in order to attend to mundane matters without interruption.

Some of the initial encounters with spirits in the lore involve a kind of formal induction or initiation. In Scottish witch-lore, the initiate stands on the foot of an elder, with the elder's hand placed over his head, and he is then able to perceive and interact with spirits. In other stories, the witch must renounce her baptismal vows in order to embark on the path unburdened by previous allegiances. In my opinion, this act of renunciation may be useful, though in solitary practice, all of it depends on the preferences of the individual.

The concept of "spiritual pacts" is vastly misunderstood. Some would say that all christians who have promised their souls to their god have entered into a kind of spiritual pact with the god of Abraham, who is historically identified as El and is descended from an entity of Mesopotamian origins who bears the same name. Make no mistake; spiritual pacts are made all around us, though not in the forms one might think. The student of folk witchcraft would be wise to take time in building relationships with spirits in order to fully understand their natures before leaping headlong into agreements that may not be worth the price.

The Old Ones

The concept of deity in folk witchcraft is complex. In the lore, there are spiritual figures who are identified as the patrons of witches, but they are numerous and can differ considerably: Diana, Holda, Freya, Aradia, Herodias, Habondia, Tana, Hecate, Selene, Baba Yaga, the King and Queen of Elphame, the Man in Black, Janicot, the Bucca, Old Hornie, Lucifer, and yes, even the Devil. The lore suggests that these are entities who, for whatever reason, see fit to teach and to lead witches. In my craft, I often refer to them simply as the Old Ones, for lack of a better term.

Why does folk witchcraft, in stark contrast to mid-century writing about witchcraft, include the Devil at all? First of all, the Devil of folklore is a distinct figure that has very little in common with the Devil of the bible. This is not the enemy of all things good, but the fiddler, the trickster, the man at the crossroads who offers a deal. The lore from which these images spring has nothing to do with the bible. Although it's true that witch-lore describes diabolic elements, such as verbally rejecting one's baptism or repeating the lord's prayer backwards, modern folk witches consider these to be methods of undoing pacts made with the christian god (as discussed previously, even that god can be a spirit who makes pacts with humans and offers rewards for a certain price). By rejecting one's baptism, the claim that the christian god once had over your soul is gone, and your ability to traverse the spirit world and seek power is no longer limited by that agreement. However, none of this is necessary, and many witches find the idea of including the Devil in their practice unsavory. My personal perspective is this: if something scares you, there may be a lesson in it. Learning cures fear better than anything else.

Through the lens of animism, we can view the Old Ones as the exalted spirits of ancient witches who rose to power through their art. In fact, Freya, who wields the distaff, may be associated with the trance-inducing tasks of fiber-work, and thereby, spirit flight.

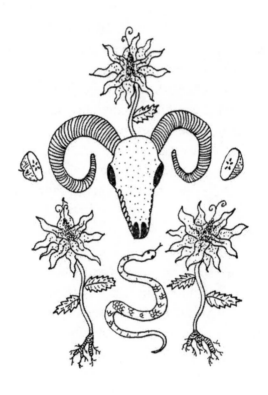

Isn't the Devil, with his animal hide and horns or antlers, suggestive of a primitive magician wearing the skin and headdress of an animal to connect with the spirit of the herd, to bridge the gap between the human and animal worlds? These beings are mysterious and potent with lore and wisdom, but most folk witches don't worship them in the sense that religious people worship gods. Instead, we work with them. We build loving, trusting relationships with them. We make offerings. We don't constantly ask for favors. In short, we treat them as great ancestors.

Practice: Finding Your Story

Purchase a notebook for your personal use. Traditionally, magical practitioners refer to these types of journals as *grimoires*, a term which shares the same root as the word *grammar*, meaning, basically, "how-to." Research the lore associated with witches, beginning with the books described in this section, and write down any charms or details that strike you as potent. You might look to lore associated with your area or with your ancestors. Try searching booksellers or libraries with keywords like *legends, folklore,* and *superstitions.* Read like a witch, eyes peeled for details that lend themselves to practical workings. Even details that seem bizarre can later be adapted into practical rituals. Use these questions to guide you:

- *How do witches achieve flight in the lore?*
- *How do witches heal and harm?*

- *What days or times are associated with witches?*
- *What spirits or ancestors preside over witches?*
- *Where do witches gather or what areas do they frequent?*
- *How do witches begin their work? What forms of initiation or dedication do these rituals take?*
- *What kinds of familiar spirits work with witches?*

Practice: Spirit Flight

If the idea of attempting spirit flight seems fantastical or outrageous to you, you're not alone. Most of us moderns have difficulty grasping the animist cosmology that would allow for the spirit to leave the body. Fortunately, with a little practical exercise, you can build this skill over time.

To begin, with your eyes closed, build up the sensation of leaving your body. With your body lying or sitting, let your spirit stand up. See your physical body below you. Feel the ground under your feet as you walk. Smell the air. Hear the wind. The witch can travel in this form to create change in and conduct observations of this plane.

A deeper method used by witches is the spirit flight unto the ethereal sabbat, which is to say, the otherworld. One simple method is to use an entrance to the otherworld that is grounded in the physical world: a cave, a hole in a tree, a stream that runs underground, a pond, a deep thicket, or another natural feature that suggests a passageway. If you are indoors, consider using a stone with a hole in it, an open window, a chimney, or a door. If you are able to do so, use a spiritual passage held in the mind's eye as an entry point.

Make your way to your chosen entrance slowly in spirit flight, holding as many of your senses as you can, then enter the otherworld. This process comes more naturally to some than others. If you have difficulty with it, consider using a blindfold or plugging your ears in order to help disassociate from your physical body and block out interference. When finished, be sure always to return to your physical body the way you came.

At first, this exercise will feel like simple visualization, but over time, the experience will deepen, and you will be able to fly at will. It may, at times, feel as if you are located in two places at once: in both your physical body and your spirit form. This is completely natural. Pay it no mind.

Some witches use lore-sourced chants to aid in this process, such as "horse and hattock, horse and go, horse and pellatis, ho, ho." The building of a rhythmic chant can act as a drum-beat and is very useful for the shifting of conscious necessary for spirit flight. If this approach appeals to you, try beginning with a clear voice, then allowing your chant to trail off and decrease in volume as you depart your body. As your chanting tapers off, let it be like a voice in the distance, far away.

Try visiting familiar places and people in your spirit-flight. Much of our witch-lore describes acts performed in the spirit body at great distances rather than face-to-face. Changes enacted in the spirit world have their natural counterparts in the physical one.

Practice: Meeting the Familiar Spirit

Eventually, at some point in your journeys to the otherworld, one of the good people will make themselves known to you. Be polite. Introduce yourself. They may appear in a form that frightens you. Don't judge a spirit solely on its initial appearance, but do judge them based on their actions. Ask for a name. You may receive an image or a word that seems illogical to you, but don't be deceived. The good people (another name for faeries and similar spirits) love riddles, and their names are often hidden in cryptograms or symbols that are meant for you alone to decipher. Write down anything you experience that might help you understand this being's identity. Analyze it carefully, then return to the spirit later and make a gesture of affection: an offering of incense or some simple words of gratitude and praise.

If you can maintain a positive relationship with this spirit over time, they will reveal secrets meant for you alone. Some practical strategies for interpreting and utilizing these gifts will be discussed in a later section of this book. For now, focus on building a friendship. Be kind. Most people are terrified of spiritual presences and proceed to banish and expel them without even getting to know them first. Although not all spirits are friendly, this kind of unprovoked rudeness and arrogance shuts off the gates to power in the otherworld. Imagine if someone showed up at your door, politely asking to use the phone to get help with a flat tire, and you chased them off your porch with a blow torch. Treat spirits with the same courtesy with which you would expect to be treated. Yes, even the spooky ones. You never know what benevolent creature is lurking behind a shadow, testing your manners before offering you the wisdom that you need to grow on your path.

Practice: Ritual Construction

Experiment by incorporating aspects of scavenged lore into your basic spirit flight practice. Do witches in your local lore frequent a particular kind of tree? Practice near a tree or holding one of its branches or nuts. Do the folkloric witches of your ancestors whisper into shells? Try holding the shell to your ear while leaving your body, or perhaps try passing into the depths of the shell. Do witches pass through keyholes? This can be another port of entry to the spirit world. Write down your favorite incantations and charms in a special section of the notebook. Get used to experimenting, revising, then experimenting again. This is part of our craft. When you find something that works particularly well for you, write down an outline of the process you used. You are now developing your own working rituals.

At this point, you may wish to try some simple charms from the lore. If you do so, during the working, focus on your spirit swelling around your body, circling the ingredients or objects you are using. Let your spirit body become much larger than your physical one, like a swirling shadow. If you've already loosened your spirit from your body before, this should be easy. Everything you touch in ritual is tinged by your spirit, which is no longer fixed to your corporeal form. The spirits you learn from, the flights you take, the lore you encounter: all of this will nourish your witch's spirit and make your work more potent.

If you struggle with feeling and holding power for a particular charm, call on your familiar. Let this spirit fill you with the current you need for the casting. If your cause is worthy of their attention, call on the Old Ones. You are connected to them by an invisible thread across the eons. They rose to power long before you came into witchcraft, and their wills are strong. They aren't servants, so be respectful, but they have chosen to become our patrons because they have a deep love of witchcraft, and they do not fail in their art.

Land

Rooting into the Land

Much of the lore associated with witches today is from the British isles. This has led people around the world to assume that their craft must utilize the herbs, seasons, and natural magics of that land in order to be legitimate. This is simply untrue. Instead, we can use the lore as a guide and teacher in order to form our own relationship with the natural world around us, wherever we are. Using what is local and connecting with one's own land is fundamental to folk witchcraft. It is also incredibly practical and deeply rewarding. Here are some questions to guide your research and growth in connecting with the land where you are:

- *What sorts of natural objects do witches use in their magic in the folklore?*
- *What role does the world of flora play in*

witches' lore?

- *What is the folkloric witch's relationship with the land?*
- *What specific formations or geographical features are significant to witches?*
- *What role does the world of fauna play in witches' lore?*
- *What sorts of animals appear to be associated with witches?*
- *What sorts of plants appear to be associated with witches?*
- *What logic governs the attribution of certain qualities to herbs?*
-

If you are lucky enough to live in a rural setting, opportunities abound for connecting with the land. A simple walk through a field, sitting beside an old tree, or gazing at a body of water can yield surprising results when paired with the spirit flight techniques shared in the previous section. If you live in a city, privacy in nature can be hard to come by. A local park, a hiking trail a couple of hours away, or even trees growing on the side of the street can suffice. All of these features of the land have unique personalities that unfold with contemplation of the symbolism inherent in them. If you can't interact with nature in person, consider taking a walk to memorize a place, then returning to it later using the spirit flight technique from the previous section of this book. Interacting with the spirits associated with local land features will help you to build a relationship with the land around you.

The Spirits of Ponds, Lakes, Streams, and Waters

Running water flows. It wears down sediment over many years. It is soft and strong at the same time. It cleanses. In Irish lore, the Danube river is associated with the goddess Danu, who is the mother of the gods. Early human settlements were often established along rivers for access to water for drinking, fishing, and cleaning. The spirits associated with running water have qualities similar to moving water itself, including the ability to "break up" blockages and wash away that which is no longer needed.

Still water is less cleansing due to its stagnant nature, but through its patience, brings forth a vast diversity of life around it. Its properties are more reflective, quiet, and nourishing. Because of the association of stagnation, still water is sometimes associated with unsavory spirits in the lore. These beings include Jenny Greenteeth, a dark faerie who grabs unsuspecting victims and drags them under the water to drown them. The Celts sank the bodies of their dead in bogs, and some have conjectured that the still, reflective surface of these places served as a portal to the otherworld.

Fresh springs emerge from reserves of water under the surface of the earth, bringing forth refreshment as well as secrets from the hidden and dark places. Springs and wells have a rich tradition in the lore. Because these are places where water emerges from the otherworld, it is common to leave gifts at sources of fresh spring water, which might involve dropping a coin or tying a ribbon to a nearby tree. A spring's life-giving, generous nature associates it with bright, amiable water spirits.

The sea is vast, beautiful, and terrifying. It can spell doom or sustain communities. Its powers are awe-inspiring and also treacherous. The spirits associated with the sea are likewise beautiful and dangerous, including the merfolk and enormous serpents. These beings are spirits of awe and destruction, and the sea is called in charms of baneful magic as well as appeals to ancient, tremendous powers that lurk beneath its depths. Because of its associations with trade and fishing, the sea is life-giving as well, though its nature is entirely unpredictable. Sea spirits, like the great oceans of the world, will do as they see fit.

Mountain, Rock, and Cave Spirits

Folklore tells us that the spirits of witches often gather on mountain peaks, in caves, and under hills. Rocks, the ancient bones of the earth, represent our connection to things long past. Our ancestors would have looked at many of the same mountainous formations that we can gaze upon today.

The principal qualities of tall rock features are farsightedness and remoteness. Like Bald Mountain, on which witches were said to gather on Walpurgis night, these areas are aloof and isolated, symbolizing a kind of solitude and unreachability that makes these spirits wild and tempestuous.

Caverns and recesses into the earth represent the opening of a door into hidden secrets from the depths. The spirits associated with these places can offer a diverse array of knowledge. Holes and tunnels can be used as entrances to the otherworld in spirit flight, and for this reason, they are associated both with faeries and with the spirits of the dead, which are often overlapping categories in the lore. The spirits of underground passages are sometimes connected with mining and human activity, like the kobold, a variety of faerie that frequents old mines. These spirits seem to enjoy the quiet and the dark and take little pleasure in human company, though they are noted in the lore to be helpful when it pleases them.

Tree Spirits

The lore of trees is old, and witches are frequently associated with these powerful beings. Trees are notable for their enormous stature among the plant kingdom; they reach both below and above, a kind of bridge between the seen and unseen worlds. Their roots plunge deep into the world of the dead, and their leaves and flowers stretch towards the sky.

The rowan is often associated with craft, cunning, and the ability to perceive magical currents at work. Its red berries are, in the lore, used for protective charms. Because the rowan's berries turn bright red in the cold, it is associated with unyielding vitality and resilience in the face of challenge. If rowan trees (or any related species) don't grow where you live, consider other trees that put out red berries in the winter. Speak with the spirits of these trees to find out their similarities and differences to the personality of the rowan.

In the lore, the birch is associated with nurturing and cleansing. It is an excellent protective spirit for children. Because its bark peels away from its base, the birch is capable of renewing itself, much like the serpent sheds its skin. Its energies are very concerned with beginnings and with allowing new things to have a proper start on their way to fruition. If birch does not grow in your area, look for other species that shed their bark in order to renew themselves, and get to know their spirits.

Few other trees have such dichotomous associations as the elder. Its berries are full of properties that build the immune system (and make a wonderful tea), but they are also full of dark juice and can smell unappetizing when dried. Often, the spirit associated with the elder is an old woman who can help or harm. It is said that, when collecting wood or fruit from the elder, it is wise to ask politely and to make some kind of offering. Because of its association with fever and illnesses that would have been dire indeed in premodern times, the elder spirit is associated with the powers of life and death. If elder does not grow where you call home, consider other trees and shrubs that produce dark and immune system-supporting fruit.

The yew tree is associated with the dead and with graveyards. In the lore, a root of a yew tree growing in a graveyard winds its way into each of the corpses buried there. What is interesting about the yew is the manner in which it grows. It is one of the most long-lived trees in the world because it spreads ever-outwards in its growth pattern, consuming the decaying portion of itself in the process. Thus, it is locked in a constant process of death and renewal. For those so inclined to meet this spirit, there is mystery in the behavior of the yew tree and those trees that act similarly.

The apple tree, like the yew tree, is also associated with the dead, since apples are, in the lore, the food of the dead. The spirit of the apple tree is generative and prolific, pouring forth its fruit in the hopes that its seeds will find their way to saplings. In late fall, the smell of an orchard is rotten-sweet from all the decaying apple flesh. Still, there is a strong fertility association in the apple tree, as anyone who has stood beneath a blooming apple tree in the spring can tell you. The hum of bees around its clean, white blossoms is magnificent. The apple spirit is sometimes associated with decision-making, since one must choose the good apples carefully. In my experience, this spirit is especially gentle and kind-natured.

The blackthorn is especially associated with the Bucca or Pucca, a shapeshifting spirit and one of the old horned deities of witchcraft. Its thorned branches and bitter fruit have been used as hedgerows to contain livestock. Its knotty wood has been used for walking sticks and wands, especially those used magically to curse or punish enemies. The blackthorn tree is closely associated with maleficium and harmful magic. In places that are not hospitable to the blackthorn, the witch can seek out trees and shrubs that are have similar barbs and black fruit.

The Spirits of Herbs and Plants

Although the student witch can easily purchase volumes upon volumes cataloging the qualities of various herbs, it is even more useful to consider the theoretical model used in assigning these attributions. In addition to the lore of specific herbs, which is an unending store of wealth, most magical herbalists are influenced by the medieval notion of the "doctrine of signatures," which entails observing the behavior of plants in order to identify the planetary attributions thereof.

In this model, plants that reach for the sun have a strong solar quality, which lends itself to workings of healing, happiness, and joy. Plants that are poisonous or develop strong root systems and return year after year have a saturnine quality, lending themselves to necromancy, cursing, and dark spirit work. Plants with barbs, thorns, or irritants are martial in nature and are useful for defense and success in competitive areas. If a plant has large, fragrant blossoms, it can be said to possess a venereal nature, potent in love, friendship, and beauty. Plants that hold watery or milky substances or enjoy the shade have a lunar quality, useful in divination and foresight. Plants with complex, small leaves or petals that flutter in the wind often have a mercurial nature, useful for learning, communication, and trade. Plants that produce prolific nuts or seeds are connected to the planetary force of Jupiter, useful for success, wealth, and influence.

It's important to note that a plant can have more than one planetary nature, so even when using the doctrine of signatures model, we can see that an individual plant spirit is more complicated and no so easily categorically defined. In addition to analysis by signature, folk witches rely on the specific lore that has amassed around certain plants over time. It would be impossible to recount here faithfully all of the plant lore a witch might need; instead, I've included a brief summary of herb lore from my own practice in the grammar portion of this book.

Some of the most infamous herbs associated with witches in the lore include atropa belladonna, datura, henbane, wormwood, mugwort, yarrow, dittany of crete, and rue, and for these herbs, it is recommended that the student witch study the lore carefully in addition to using signature analysis and talking with the plant's spirit.

Atropa belladonna, henbane, and datura are sometimes identified as ingredients in the fabled flying ointment used by medieval witches in order to travel to the sabbat. Today, we know that these plants all contain compounds that can contribute to excitatory states when used topically and in moderation. The witch who wishes to experiment with these properties is well-advised to purchase the salves of experienced herbalists. Many witches who are skilled in the herbal arts make and sell their own ointments for very reasonable prices. The effects of these unguents, when made properly, are not inebriating, but merely loosen the spirit from the body in a subtle way. They can be a great aid to spirit flight, but they will not do it for you.

A very safe unguent can be made by even the novice herbalist by infusing 4 tbsp of mugwort and 4 tbsp of wormwood in one cup of sweet almond oil in a 200 degree oven for four hours. After the oil has cooled, strain the mixture with cheesecloth to remove the plant matter, then measure the resulting oil and add beeswax in a ratio of one part wax to five parts oil. Reheat in a clean pan to melt the wax, then pour into a jar and allow to cool before using. Apply to the chest, neck, back, and pulse points to aid in spirit flight.

Most commonly, herbs are used to prepare infusions. The application of hot water to dried herbs is known to awaken and vivify their properties. Skullcap tea is excellent for anxiety. Passionflower is a wonderful sleep-aid. Peppermint is soothing for an ailing stomach. White willow can calm a headache. Magical infusions allow the witch to savor the fullest flavor of the herb and absorb its magical properties. (As always, be sure to use *edible* herbs for this purpose.)

A tincture is another common herbal preparation useful to witches. To make a tincture, mix one part dried herb with two parts vodka and seal in a bottle of jar tightly. Allow to set in a warm place for four weeks, then strain the plant matter from the alcohol and funnel into a dropper bottle. One dose of a tincture made from healthful herbs is 5-7 drops. For magical use, the tincture can be used to dress a variety of objects. The alcohol dissolves quickly, leaving only traces of the plant.

A magical incense can make for simple and satisfying spell-work All one needs is an open fire, a piece of hot charcoal in a safe burner, or even a votive candle burning in the bottom of a cauldron or bowl. As the herbs burn and the smoke rises, the intention of the witch spreads and travels upon the air.

Lastly, powders can play an important role in magical herbalism. A mortar and pestle or electric herb grinder are excellent tools for this process. After selecting a few herbs aligned with the planetary energies corresponding to the magical intention, grind the herbs to a fine powder. This powder can be used on objects, blown toward the target's front door, or applied to oneself.

With all herbal preparations, be sure to pay careful attention to any potential side effects or toxicity. Contrary to popular belief, not all herbal medicine is "free of side-effects." In fact, most of our medicines today are derived from compounds derived from plants. These are powerful beings with potent spirits, and with a little knowledge and care, they can be great allies.

Along with a horned animal skull to represent the King of Elphame or Old Hornie, some witches may wish to honor the Queen of Elphame or Queen of the Sabbat by placing fresh flora of the season on the altar or working space.

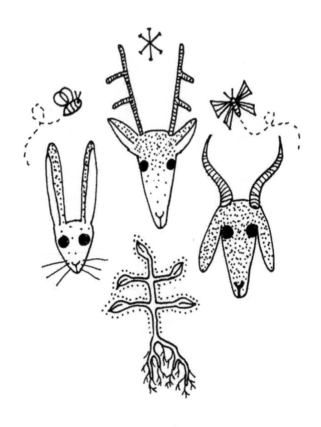

Animal Spirits

Certain animals are associated with witches more than others, though these vary in the lore of different cultures. Frequently, cats, dogs, serpents, hares, bats, toads, spiders, and birds top the list. What is interesting about these animals as a group is their incredible utility to humans living in a rural setting. Most of them prey on vermin that spread disease among humans. There's no better solution to a fly problem than allowing spiders to set up shop. Mice on the farm? Adopt a lovely barn cat. Pests invading the corn crib and ruining the winter stores? Be sure not to kill the snake living under the shed. The presence of toads, with their absorbent skin and love of moisture, indicates a local ecosystem low in chemical pollutants.

Creatures that burrow beneath the earth, principally snakes and hares, are strongly associated with witchcraft in the lore. Because these animals are capable of traveling below the earth, they can be said to occupy two realms in the same way that trees stretch between the earth and sky. These creatures are also elusive, excellent at hiding, and so they are associated with both secret knowledge and good fortune when they are spotted. In the same way, creatures that swim or fly are associated with their principle element, and the spirits of these creatures will bear the marks of their behavior in the wild. Watching animals closely is a great way to begin connecting with their spirits.

Horned animals, especially, are associated with witches in the lore. Stags, rams, and goats bearing horns and hooves are prey animals hunted and eaten by our ancestors. The many cave paintings of horned human figures depict our symbiotic relationship with these creatures and the magical efforts undertaken by early humans to connect with them in order to ensure survival. Many traditional witches seek to connect with this entity known as the Devil or King of Elphame in his aspect of Lord of Animals by placing horns, antlers, or the skull of one of these animals on an altar or in the center of a space used for workings.

One common practice among witches in the lore is the ability to travel outside of the body in animal form. Even the myth of the werewolf is deeply connected to witchcraft in folklore, usually seen by witch hunters as one particular form that witchcraft could take. It's difficult not to think of the animal dances performed by animist cultures when one thinks of witches transforming into animals in order to conduct their workings. In practical terms, taking on the form of a particular animal during spirit flight may be a way to utilize the qualities associated with that creature's spirit. This works best with spirits with whom the witch has already built a strong relationship.

Sabbats, Seasons, and Tides

We know the seasons not only by the temperature, but by the behavior of the creatures that live on our land. Wherever you live, there are tell-tale signs that distinct seasons have come and gone. What plants flower first? Last? What insects are the first to become prolific when the temperature allows for it? Are there animals that only appear at certain times of year? Watch your landscape closely, and study it. The way life ebbs and flows during the year is closely associated with the sabbats observed in folk craft. With that said, the seasons under which much of the witch lore we recognize developed were four in number: winter, spring, summer, and fall; the resting, cleansing, growing, and reaping tides, respectively. Let's take a closer look at some of the dates associated with traditional craft lore as inherited from the British isles. (For examples of sabbat rituals, see the Grammar section of this book.)

All Hallow's Eve

Of all the sabbats, perhaps the most frequently associated with witchcraft in the popular imagination is All Hallow's Eve. This sabbat falls at the end of October and heralds the end of fall and the beginning of winter. On this night, spirits of the dead and those representing the dark half of the year are said, in the lore, to roam free. Some magical operations associated with this sabbat include the dumb supper, which is a dinner set in silence in honor of the dead, and the casting of the clew, which is a rite involving a ball of string associated with the Scottish Witch Queen, Nicneven. The ball is tossed into a dark place, such as a room or a cauldron, and the string is pulled slowly while calling to her spirit, which is fabled to hold the other end.

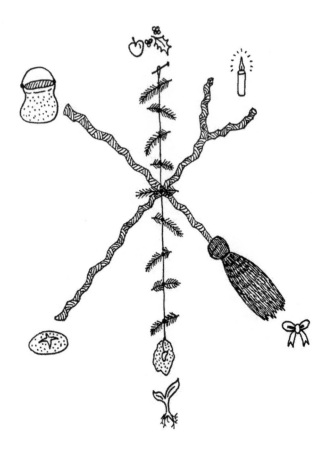

Yule and The Twelfth Night

Traditionally, Yule was more of a season than a holiday, lasting twelve days, and festivities were quite extensive. The Twelfth Night marks the twelfth day after Christmas, the pinnacle of the winter season. In the lore, there are stories of spirits riding the cold winds in a great horde during this dark time of the year. There are also Yule spirits associated with rewards and punishments for the choices we make during the year. These include not only the well-known St. Nicholas, but Befana and Krampus as well. Rituals associated with The Twelfth Night in the lore include the telling of ghost stories and the wassail, which involves singing and offering cider to apple trees in exchange for a good orchard harvest.

Candlemas

This sabbat falls at the beginning of February and marks the end of winter and the beginning of spring. As its name suggests, this holiday is strongly associated with fire, warmth, and light. In Scottish lore, this is the date on which the hag of winter, named the Cailleach, decides how much more cold and snow will befall the land. If the weather is fair, the Cailleach will head out to gather firewood, thus enabling her to stay warm in the midst of more ill weather. If the weather is cloudy, the Cailleach is said to sleep, unable to work the magic necessary to prolong the freeze. It was common, at one time, to bless candles for later use on this date.

May Eve

Also celebrated as Beltane and Walpurgis Night, the last day of April is a sabbat in observation of the end of spring and the beginning of summer. On this night, bonfires were lit for good fortune, sometimes carried into the house to light hearths and candles. The ashes of these fires were said to have protective properties. Early in the morning on May 1st, young women would sneak out to wash their faces with dew in the hopes of enhancing their beauty. This was also a time to dance the maypole, which is descended from the May bush, a thorny shrub decorated with ribbons. In Scottish lore, the beginning of May marks the time when the hag of winter transforms into the maiden of summer. In addition to All Hallow's Eve, May Eve is a key sabbat for witches, and it is a propitious time of year for spirit flight and festivities celebrating the turning of the seasons.

Midsummer

The peak of the summer season, which falls in the latter half of June, is a key time in the lore for the beings known as faeries, which is to say, the otherwordly spirits of the ancestors. This is the turning point at which days begin to shorten and nights begin to lengthen. This is also said to be a propitious time for gathering herbs and blessing them for magical use later in the year. The lore tells us that, on this night, people would leave offerings of milk and bread to the faeries in exchange for good luck.

Lammas

Lammas means *loaf mass*, and it refers to a celebration of the first of the harvest. It falls at the end of July. When farmers would reap the initial fruits of their labors, this date marked payment due to the landowners. It also marks the end of summer and the beginning of fall. On this sabbat, it is traditional to bake a loaf of bread, divide it into four pieces, and leave the pieces at the four corners of a property in order to bring good fortune throughout the harvest season.

The Moon and the Esbats

Another important time for witches is the night of the full moon. *Esbat* is a term derived from French sources, and it usually refers to a time of playfulness and frolic. The light of the full moon made it possible for our ancestors to hunt at night and to conduct rituals outdoors, which would be very difficult on a pitch-black night. While not all witches honor the full moons with ritual, I would hazard a guess to say that most do. There is a tremendous amount of lore associated with the moon, and it makes good sense for folk witches, whose practices are rooted in lore, to honor the powerful currents of the spirit world operating at this time.

Practice: Learning the Land

Using the basic method for spirit flight from earlier exercises, try to identify and locate some local land spirits. What natural formations, bodies of water, or old trees are in your own neighborhood? If you are uncomfortable going into a trance state out in public, take a stroll around the area, memorize it, then return to it later in spirit form by using your spirit flight technique. Try to make contact with the spirit ruling this place. As always, be kind and respectful, and write down in your grimoire any images, words, or impressions that come to you during this working.

Practice: Plant Spirits

Determine some key useful plants that grow in your area. If you live near a college or university with an agriculture or botany program, their website may maintain listings with photographs to help you identify these plants. Next, go out on your own, and attempt to find them in your area. If a particular plant with a recognizable trait seems to grow around your property with abandon, try to identify it. Today, there are even applications available for the smartphone that can help you to identify plants around you. Once you know the name and properties of a plant in your area, conduct workings to introduce yourself to the plant's spirit. Get to know its nature, and of course, write down any mysteries it reveals to you.

Practice: Shapeshifting

Obtain a physical representation of a wild animal that lives in your area. Bird feathers, sun-bleached bones, antlers, bits of hair, moth wings, a wasp nest, a cicada shell: all can be used as physical objects to connect you with an animal's spirit. Hold the piece of your chosen animal in your hand. Begin your spirit flight process, but this time, emerge in the form of the animal you chose. Realize its body carefully: feel its posture, its fur (if it has fur), its senses. Travel in this form to see and learn things you would not be able to experience in your normal spirit form.

Practice: Laying the Compass, Ring, or Circle

Many witches align themselves with the powers of the land around them before powerful spell-work by casting a circle, a ring, or a compass. This identifies and locates the witch in proximity to the four cardinal directions and the powers they represent. In the lore, we encounter witches dancing or walking in a circle, the presence of a "faerie ring" acting as a portal to a hidden world, and circles laid out with specific names and sigils representing different operations. In folk witchcraft, this simple magical act is sometimes called "laying the ring." This can be done simply by dragging a forked branch (sometimes called a stang, which is another term for distaff) around a circle, saying:

Thus I lay the ring about.

Thout a thout and tout a tout.
Powers East, South, West, and North,
By my craft, I call thee forth.

The associations of the four directions closely corresponds to the lore surrounding the four winds. Boreas is the Greek name for the North wind, the spirit of cold and winter. Eurus is the name of the East wind, associated with the dawn. Notus is the name of the South wind, spirit of heat and storm. Zephyrus is the spirit of the West wind, bringer of gentle breezes and nourishing rains.

Practice calling to the four winds. Call them simply, by name, facing the direction from which they ride.

Coniuro te spiritus Boreas.
Coniuro te spiritus Eurus.
Coniuro te spiritus Notus.
Coniuro te spiritus Zephyrus.

In the old Greek lore, they are sometimes depicted as horses or horsemen. Visualize them as great clouds in the shape of horses billowing towards you in the distance, answering your call. Let them empower your craft.

Practice: The Sabbat

By studying the land carefully in connection to the lore, you should now have an idea of the sacred times in your own area and how they connect with the tides of nature. Begin to observe these times with special rituals planned for the occasion. There are some in the grammar section of this book if you need a place to start. Do not feel that these rituals need to be grandiose or complex in nature; simply lighting a candle, speaking a few words from the heart, and leaving an offering outdoors can be a marvelous way to honor the spirits at work around us at these times. You may, if you wish, conduct spirit flight during this time in order to commune with the spirits of witches and the ancestors of witches who are said to fly about and celebrate. Even if you don't, do not be surprised if you have incredibly vivid dreams on these nights. Witches often find themselves swept up during these special times of the year to celebrate in spirit form with our kind. These dreams are powerful experiences, a kind of special invitation to those who commemorate the sabbats and make offerings to the spirits.

The Familiar Spirit

Beginning Spirit Work

At last, we come to the most crucial strand of initiation for the solitary folk witch. This threshold is a mystery more personal than the others and often kept private. I can't share with you the specific guidance and teachings of my familiar spirits, and nor should you share yours with anyone you don't know on a deeply intimate level (and even then, sometimes, it's best not to speak of such things, especially if the spirit has bound you to silence, as they sometimes do). We can, however, discuss dealings with spirits in general terms. Moreover, we can dissect some of the concrete methods for analyzing, interpreting, and implementing the secrets shared with us by familiar spirits. Here are some questions to guide your personal explorations with spirits:

- *Is this spirit willing to share its name? Why or why not?*

- *Has the spirit shared any words or images that might contain a kind of name?*
- *What does this spirit's name appear to mean on a surface level?*
- *What does the name sound like? What words might be similar to the sound of its name?*
- *How would you describe the sounds of the words in its name? Are they sharp, soft, nasal, guttural, airy, hard? What might this mean?*
- *How does this spirit appear to you? What sensations accompany its appearance?*
- *What might its perceived form be interpreted to mean?*
- *What kinds of things does this spirit do when it appears? Is it walking, talking, flying, etc.?*
- *Where and when does the spirit seem more likely to appear?*

Because the witch can be said to possess a kind of dual-citizenship in the spirit world and the physical world, narratives concerning witches have often portrayed us as untrustworthy or duplicitous, having a mysterious connection to invisible forces. In reality, learning the etiquette of the spirit world and building positive relationships with its denizens can actually teach us something of who we ought to be in our mundane lives and how to best treat one another.

Dreams, Visions,
and the Black Book

The primary reason for the witch to connect with the familiar spirit is to learn, which is a form of love. In the lore, we often find mention of the "black book" in which witches sign their names in exchange for power and from which the spirits teach, sharing bits of magical knowledge with the practitioner over time. Seasoned witches learn that, although there are many grimoires and magical manuals in circulation, some of which are quite old, the legendary "black book" of the lore does not exist physically, but spiritually.

How can that be? How can the source of ongoing learning and ritual in witchcraft be non-existent in the physical world? The answer is surprisingly simple. If you wish to understand the true meaning of the black book of art, meditate upon this question: How did the witches and sorcerer of old arrive at their ABAXACATABAXes and ASKEI KATASKEIs? How did the authors of the medieval and renaissance grimoires discover these now famous magical formulae?

The old grimoires were of course constructed from the workings of individual practitioners under the tutelage of their own spirit guides. Each of us has access to the black book. It is the current of knowledge opened by connection to the familiar spirit. Its words of power, its rites, its laws and lessons: these treasures all flow from the initiatory current of the familiar spirit. From the perspective of a folk witch, those who follow every detail in some medieval grimoire and expect to receive the same results as the original writer have, in many ways, missed the point. To stumble across a great magical book in your research is certainly a kind of gift and a door to initiation, but to attempt its rites without a connection to the spirit from which it proceeds is like planting seeds in the desert.

By now, you may have some idea of why you have been studying the lore and communing with spirits rather than following a prescribed ritual structure dictated by the author; without being able to perceive and receive wisdom from the otherworld, the physical acts of witchcraft are only dead husks. By establishing a strong connection to the initiatory currents of the lore, the land, and the spirits around us, we are able to tap into the roots of folk craft. We understand both the how and the why of witchcraft. The personal grimoire, as a physical replica of the spiritual black book, contains the witch's dreams, visions, and experiences of the spiritual world alongside the collected lore and charms from her research.

Intentionally opening the black book of the sabbat through ritual can be an invigorating experience. There is a charm for this purpose in the Grammar section of this book. This working is conducted in spirit flight. The witch accesses the otherworld through an appropriate point of entry, then calls to the old ones using a spoken charm. There, the witch will be invited to an enclave of knowledge that can only be accessed by those acccepted by the spirits. The black book is closed to the profane.

Other Varieties of Familiar Spirits

By now, you have likely made contact with spirits of flora and fauna and perhaps even a spirit who was drawn to you by certain shared qualities. Familiar spirits can come from many different sources and in many varieties. Most witches interact with spirits related closely to natural creatures and landscapes or those who appear to the individual witch spontaneously. Still, there are other places to find them.

The lore is rich with proverbial catalogues of familiar spirits, often described as "faeries," "brownies," or "elves," who frequent human habitations and offer aid in exchange for strange currencies. The Folletino Rosso, loosely translated as "Red Goblin," is a spirit described in Leland's *Aradia*. He dwells in small, round stones, and can be conjured with a specific charm to bring luck and good fortune.

The Wag at the Wa' is a Scottish brownie who dwells beside kitchen fires in a cast iron crook, a metal hook used to hang pots. He is conjured by swinging the object to and fro over a flame, after which he will take up residence in the metal curve, his favorite armchair. The Hobbitrot is associated with holed stones and the fiber arts. She appears as an elderly woman with a long lip, engorged from wetting thread with her mouth. She prizes hard work and good manners, and she is especially friendly toward unmarried women.

Some grimoires, perhaps most notably the many goetic texts derived from Weyer's *Pseudomonarchia Daemonium,* detail spirits' names, sigils, and characteristics. These spirits are referred to commonly as demons, but a close examination of their sources reveals a more complex origin story. Take, for example, the spirit Astaroth. This entity has, for its sigil, a pentagram with additional lines and details. It appears to be a garbled form of Astarte or Ishtar, a Mesopotamian star goddess who is also closely associated with the five-pointed star. Similarly, Flauros or Haures appears, both in name and in sigil, to be derived from the Egyptian god Horus. Although it's difficult to say with complete accuracy how these spirits came to be reclassified as demons, we do know that the Romans would, before conquering a city, bind its patron gods and ancestor spirits in ritual to prevent them coming to the people's aid, and this imprisonment and denigration of other cultures' spirits seems to have been inherited by the catholic church. Many of the grimoires describing these "demons" were written by priests and monks experimenting with magic, and these spirits were summoned by means of threats, punishment, and torment within an enclosed vessel. If you experiment with the spirits of the Goetia, do so kindly and respectfully, but also do so with a sealed magical circle as a barrier between you and the spirit, since centuries of harassment and enslavement have not made these spirits friendlier toward humans.

Witches are also noted in our lore to work with the spirits of the dead. Those who pass beyond our world are, in the lore, transformed into something that is still sentient, but no longer quite the same person in some ways. The faerie lore of celtic cultures is, essentially, suggestive of a cult of the dead, of ancestors beneath the land who rise up in spirit form and demand regular offerings. These spirits can offer a kind of wisdom that bridges the gap between the human and spirit worlds. However, just because they were once human does not necessarily mean they are friendly towards the living. The residual entity that remains when a person passes is not, in my opinion, exactly the same as who the person was in life. They often still express love and fondness for family and friends, and they may appear in their physical form or use their voice, but their priorities are now quite different. They are no longer a part of the dance of life and no longer hold the same vital, survival-seeking energy as they did in life. Struggle seems to be placed with surrender, feeling with some degree of indifference. Consciousness seems to fade or maybe disappear entirely, leaving behind a loosely associated collection of attributes that we define as "Tom" or "Ellen" or "Piper." What is left is like a negative space where the person once was. It is a hollow form in the exact shape of the absence we are able to perceive, like a mold from which the original has been removed. Summoning these spirits works best when you have one or more personal items related to them, or better yet, people who remember them, present during the conjuring.

Another alternative source for familiar spirits is local legend and place names. These spirits are sometimes referred to as genii loci (the spirits of place), and they can be connected to land features, as we have already discussed, but they can also be connected to mythical creatures like the Jersey Devil or the Goatman. In the absence of local legends, look to the names of rivers, old roads, and mountains near where you live, as these can often contain a clue to a local spirit's name and principal qualities.

The Language of Spirits

Understanding the language of spirits and interpreting their messages is more of an art than a science. Some spirits seem to announce their names and teachings quite clearly, while others can be difficult to understand. Two key methods for communication are the use of automatic drawing and speech. These methods were formally introduced by an occultist named Austin Osman Spare, and they have become staples in many forms of traditional craft, though their origins are far older, as evidenced by the detailed spirit workings recorded in the grimoire tradition. For drawing, the hand is inscribed with a symbol or a series of words describing the nature of the entity, then the hand is given over to the spirit for use as a temporary vessel. The witch allows the hand to move freely with a pen and paper, focusing the presence of the spirit entirely in the hand.

Later, these drawings and words are analyzed for hidden meanings and reconfigured into more convenient and duplicatable sigils and words of power.

Automatic speech, sometimes referred to as glossolalia, entails allowing the spirit to move your lips and mouth in order to form utterances. Beginning with even a simple chant related to witch-lore, such as *Io Evohe, Io Evohe, Io Evohe*, can shift and reconfigure during the automatic session to form new sounds and words. These should be recorded, written down, or memorized for analysis later.

Abjuration and Banishing

Unfortunately, not all spirits are friendly. It's rarer than most people think, but some spirits enjoy inflicting pain. Most spiritual entities simply have work to do that we may not understand completely; they are tasked with the proliferation of some plant or animal or substance that has an important role to play in the world around us. If we are somehow in the way, that isn't necessarily the spirit's fault, and it doesn't indicate a malevolent entity, per se. That said, if a witch perceives physical weakening or harm when interacting with a spirit, there are numerous methods in the lore for asking, or if necessary, forcing it to cease its activity.

The abjuration is the equivalent to a warning given before proceeding with more severe approaches. Technically, it is a renunciation of any invitation given to the spirit and of any meaningful agreement or relationship. At this point, the witch should have acquired at least one familiar spirit and built a relationship with the Old Ones. It is common to use the names of powerful spirits with whom you have a strong connection when making the abjuration. In the grimoires, practitioners of magic would clearly and loudly identify themselves as the descendants, servants, or initiates of a particular entity (for christian grimoires, this entity was always the trinity), then perform the abjuration in their names. This alerts the offending spirit that you are not to be trifled with and gives them an opportunity to depart before more serious consequences befall them. On a more subtle level, this conjures the presence of spiritual allies to bring the power of the offending spirit into balance.

Usually, when a spirit realizes that a person is not easy prey, they move on. Be sure to mean it before using an abjuration, since many friendly spirits can appear frightening upon first impression. A spirit who has been abjured is unlikely to reveal its secret teachings to you, work with you in the future, or come to your aid in a time of need.

Very, very rarely, a spirit may resist abjuration and rise to the challenge offered by the witch. In this case, there are numerous methods for containing and punishing the spirit. The first task is to discern the name and sigil of the spirit in question. If interacting with the spirit fails to yield an encoded name, this can be discerned via divinatory techniques, such as scrying or cartomancy. Assigning letters to the variables used in a form of divination will allow fate to deliver the letters to the witch, who then must combine them intuitively to form the name. The forms in which the spirit appears can also be combined creatively to form a symbol representing the spirit.

A spirit trap, which can be any object that seals completely, is often used by placing an offering and the spirit's sigil within it and then closing the top once the spirit is conjured inside. An appropriate offering can be determined by the appearance and nature of the spirit, but usually, precious stones or coins will suffice. This trap should then be removed from your property and buried somewhere (possibly on the land of someone you don't like very much). This type of magic operates on the principle of transference.

Another method for punishing malevolent spirits is torment via sympathetic magic. Spirits are every bit as susceptible to sympathetic charms as human beings are. Burning, drowning, crushing, or suffocating a fetish designed for the spirit with the being's name or image upon it is a deeply painful experience that spirits would prefer to avoid.

Lastly, problematic spirits can be imprisoned permanently by the vigilance of the Old Ones. This can be accomplished via a box. The six interior walls of the box are inscribed with the names and signs of one of the Old Ones with whom you have a strong connection. By placing the spirit's name or sigil within the box and sealing it, the entity is imprisoned forever (or until some unlucky fool releases it).

Sigils and Incantatory Formulae

There are many ways to derive incantations, signs, and symbols from the names and utterances of spirits. The resulting sigils and incantations can be employed formally in rituals or as charms to be used for everyday magical needs. These methods build on the sigilization work of Austin Osman Spare and have proven themselves to be a tried and true body of techniques in traditional craft.

It is important to understand that a spirit's name and its mysteries are not necessarily universal, but specific to the witch with whom they are shared. This is not so different from a person who goes by "Dr. Jones" at the office, "Sarah" when with her partner, and "Mommy" with her children. These names all refer to the same person, and similarly, the same spirit can reveal different names to different individuals who are able to perceive them without any contradiction.

Take a spirit's utterance, even something simple like "I give wisdom of the air." One can interpret the words of this phrase as pertaining to the element air. The sounds of this phrase can be deconstructed and simplified by repeated changing into something like the following:

I give wisdom of the air
Igiv isdomof thair
Yg Viz D'mar

We have now arrived at a workable spirit name. We know from its passphrase that this spirit is a teaching spirit whose nature may be useful for purposes of divination and augury. If this spirit appears in a particular form, we also have some images that can serve as other keys to understand its personality and attributes. We can use drawings of these images along with the spirit name, transcribed in a magical alphabet, to arrive at a workable sigil to represent the spirit.

This image can be further simplified into a smaller sigil for convenient use.

Lastly, we can use the technique of "galdr" to derive an incantation to conjure this spirit's presence. This tradition is derived from the singing of the Germanic runes. The process is flexible and intuitive. Simply draw out the consonants with additional syllables until you arrive at a series of utterances loosely based on the sounds in the name. Using this hypothetical spirit name as an example, the result may look something like the following:

Yg Viz D'mar
Yayig Eeja Avee Azay Deum Ama Er

Chanting or intoning the conjuration above can be used to summon the spirit or its qualities to the witch to empower spells, align with the spirit's qualities, or to commune with this entity during a session of spirit flight.

Conjuring Spirits

Unlike ceremonial magic and other modern forms of "high" magic, folk witchcraft does not seek to constrain spirits within prisons or enslave them to do our bidding. Instead, we seek partnership with the spirit world in order to achieve mutually agreeable goals. This means that our methods and approaches to conjuring spirits to appear and communicate with us are inherently different and more intuitive, using simple rituals and heart-felt offerings.

Most spirits are drawn to welcoming gestures and good manners. They can also be assuaged to involve themselves in human matters through offerings of incense, praise, bread, fruit, wine, honey, milk, and butter. The witch who is willing to pay attention to the little details and make regular offerings to the spirits will find that the good people remember and reciprocate kindness. Things that are offered openly and simply without any expectation of a "favor" in the early stages of spirit contact will be more meaningful and will lay the groundwork for years of friendly collaboration.

To begin spirit conjuration, consider constructing an effigy, hand-sculpted statue, or arrangement of items associated with the spirit, such as bones, dried plant materials, stones, and so on. If you have developed a sigil and incantation, use these as well. Place the items within

a triangle drawn on a surface with flour or laid out with twigs gathered from the ground. Set incense or any other offerings around the triangle to entice the spirit to appear to you, and focus on loosening your spirit from your body in order to awaken your witch's sight.

Many spoken charms exist for conjuring spirits, some quite old, but the folk witch would be wise to avoid those incantations that use threats of fire or torment to evoke an entity. How would you feel if a stranger called you up, asked for a favor, and threatened to set you on fire if you didn't drive over to their house this very minute? Spirit compulsion is not a difficult task for the skilled folk witch, but it violates trust and burns bridges. What is far more challenging and more rewarding is building relationships with spirits based on kindness, generosity, and good manners.

Fetishes and Vessels

Familiar spirits who frequently offer aid or wisdom to the witch can be honored with a sacred object in which their spirit can temporarily dwell. These are sometimes called spirit houses, vessels, or fetishes, and they can take as many forms as the creative witch can imagine. Most commonly, witches use small carvings or sculptures with vaguely human features and shapes. Some use spirit bottles (these are meant to honor the spirit rather than trapping it, which is a different operation). These objects can be adorned with signs relevant to the spirit's nature, and they can also be filled with herbs, small objects, and pieces of paper with relevant sigils in order to draw the spirit into the dwelling place. Placed on the witch's altar or in a shrine, these fetishes can invite the spirit to pursue a more intimate connection with the witch.

Offerings appropriate to the spirit

usually include candles, incense, words of praise, and other forms of heart-felt affection. All of these will invite the spirit to take up residence and encourage a friendly relationship between the witch and the familiar spirit. Expensive gifts are unnecessary.

Likewise, the idea of "sacrificing" an animal, though certainly used by our pagan ancestors, is not a part of our modern worldview. In reality, many cultures

who made sacrifices would then eat the animals they slaughtered, so we can view the killing act as a spiritualized celebration of the livestock cycle and a way of imbibing a portion of the spirit. Most of us cannot begin to understand the world in which live sacrifice made sense, and the spirits who are drawn to us would probably be similarly shocked at the ridiculousness of such a violent gesture made by a modern witch who did not grow up in a viking village in which the blot rite was commonplace. So please, don't kill some poor creature in an attempt to please a spirit.

Many traditional witches use some form of the cakes and wine, houzle, or "red meal" rite as part of regular sabbat work, which is a modern ritual popularized by the writings of Robert Cochrane. The houzle is certainly descended from the sacrifices made by our pagan ancestors, but interpreted through a contemporary lens. In sharing sustenance with the spirit world, a powerful connection is forged between the witch and the ancestors, the faeries, and the dead. A simple folk version of this rite is provided in the grammar at the end of this book as part of the sabbat and esbat rituals.

Practice: Calling to the Familiar

Once you have established a connection to a particular familiar spirit, ask the spirit how it would like to be called for spiritual work. You will likely be provided with some words or gestures that relate to this spirit's particular nature. Write these in your grimoire, and use them when you wish to call the spirit to you in times of need or to further empower your charms. You may wish to incorporate the words and images received into the following example (the bull, dog, horn, and paw here are specific to the forms of the spirit perceived as "Vinegar Tom"):

> *I conjure thee, O familiar spirit*
> *Vinegar Tom.*
> *Come, Vinegar Tom, by and by.*
> *Come by the bull and by the dog.*
> *Come by the horn and by the paw.*
> *Come, Vinegar Tom, by and by.*

Practice: The Witch's Altar

Set aside a space in your home to honor the spirits and the Old Ones. This space can include, if you wish, a horned animal skull (fauna) to represent the King of Elphame and dried or fresh flowers or fruit (flora) to represent the Queen of Elphame. Place any fetishes on this altar as well. Use candles, incense, and natural objects, such as semiprecious stones, to honor these spirits and welcome them. Once you find an arrangement that is pleasing to you, record it in your personal grimoire. Spend a little time with your altar every so often, and don't be ashamed to speak with the spirits there, offering words of kindness and appreciation. In some lore, it is said that spirits don't care much for "thank you" since it sounds dismissive, but praising their good qualities and speaking other simple words of appreciation can do no wrong.

Practice: Calling to the Old Ones

Read the folklore and mythology of one of the deities or mythological ancestors associated with witchcraft. Learn what animals, plants, objects, and places are associated with this particular ancestor. Use these in order to arrive at a workable conjuration that speaks to the particular qualities of this entity. If you wish, you may use the following example to organize your invocation:

> *I conjure thee, O great one known*
> *by the name of Aradia,*
> *teacher and guide of witches past.*
> *Aradia of the rue,*
> *Aradia of the water, wine, and salt,*
> *Aradia of the people,*
> *Aradia of the sun and moon,*
> *Aradia the pilgrim,*
> *Aradia, who flies above the trees,*
> *Aradia, of the wind,*
> *Come, O great one,*

and bless me with your presence.

Grammar

Preface to the Grammar

The rituals and charms in this portion of the book are my own, and although they are sourced in the lore, I have experimented with them and adapted them to my use over time. I don't claim them to be the arcane secrets of some ancient cultus sworn to secrecy. They are the result of research, experimentation, and deep spirit work with my familiars. In the style of a true grimoire, I present them without exercises, explanation, or footnotes. Feel free to use them and adapt them to your own purposes. Even better, look up the lore from which they spring, and derive your own working version of these old charms under the guidance of your own familiar spirits. In my experience, witchcraft is work. It is something we do. Go ahead and get your hands dirty.

Unless otherwise specified, the rituals in my grammar are performed in a candle-lit room away from intrusion and interruption. It may be useful to light enough candles to be able to see and read incantations before beginning. These rituals may be performed as simply or as ornately as needed. The ring may or may not be cast before the working, and items and ingredients may be substituted with what is local and affordable.

Tools of the Art

All tools are possible. No tools are necessary. The following tools represent those that I have used most frequently, but this is in no way a comprehensive listing, nor do I use all of these tools in every or even most rituals.

The witch's knife serves to cut, to carve, to sever, and at times, to stir. It is a practical knife used both magically and physically in ritual. It should be simple and distinct from a kitchen knife, having a handle made of wood, antler, bone, horn, or some other natural substance.

The stang is a staff or wand that is forked on one end. It is descended from the distaff and is used in spirit flight, to lay magical boundaries, direct power, and as a portable altar representing horned deities.

The besom is a broom made in the old style (round rather than flat). It is used to asperge or sprinkle water about the compass to cleanse it before inviting the Old Ones.

The cauldron is a large, cast-iron pot used to contain water, incense, or other ingredients used in ritual. It should be large enough to accommodate the bristled end of the besom.

The central altar may be permanent or portable, and it should be made up of a horned animal skull, teeth, bones, or feathers to represent fauna and the King of Elphame. Flowers, branches, twigs, or fruit of the season should be set around the animal parts to represent the powers of flora and the Queen of Elphame. This portion of the altar should be furthest from the working space and should be graced by three candles, the center-most candle glowing from behind the skull, representing the light of the Horned One, the two peripheral candles touching the foliage to represent the Queen. For simplicity's sake, one candle may be used instead of three.

To Lay a Simple Ring

This simplified circle requires only a stang. In the absence of a workable stang, the witch may circumambulate with a lit candle instead. Move around in a circle to mark the ring, either on the ground or in the air.

Before me,
behind me,
on my right hand,
on my left hand,
above me,
and below me,
I conjure thee, O ring of art.

To Lay a More Ornate Ring

This circle ritual requires a candle, a cauldron or bowl of water, a besom, a dish of salt, incense, matches, a knife, and a stang.

Hold hand over the dish of salt.

> *I conjure thee, O creature of salt. Be thou pure and potent as the bones of the earth.*

Dip salt into water using knife.

> *I conjure thee, O creature of water. Be thou pure and potent as the roiling sea.*

Light candle.

> *I conjure thee, O creature of fire. Be thou pure and potent as living flame.*

Light the incense.

*I conjure thee, O creature of incense. Be thou
pure and potent as the voice ethereal.*

Dip the besom in salt water, then asperge about
the space in a circle.

*I cleanse and purify this space with earth and
water, that it be fit for the workings of my
craft.*

Carry incense about the room, fanning to
disperse.

*I cleanse and purify this space with fire and
air, that it be fit for the workings of my craft.*

Take up the stang, and drag around in a circle
to demarcate the ring (widdershins, or
counterclockwise, for dark work; deosil, or
clockwise, for light work).

*I conjure thee, O ring of art,
by the North, East, South, and West.
Be thou fit for the Old Ones, and be thou
an emblem of the ancient alignment
of those above and those below.*

A Simple Sabbat Rite

This sabbat ritual is designed to celebrate the agricultural festivals of our ancestors. What follows is an outline ritual that can be supplemented with specific rites for each of the sabbats, all detailed in the pages following this ritual. The simple sabbat rite here requires only a glass of spirits or juice, a candle, and any ingredients specific to the rite of the season. A simple altar may be utilized, being composed of flora and fauna beside a single candle (bone and dried flower, tooth and root, feather and seeds, shell and moss, etc.).

Take up the candle, light it, and walk around the space clockwise.

> *Here I set the ring about,*
> *Thout a thout and tout a tout.*

Set the candle upon the altar, and call to the
Old Ones.

> *Io Regina Pigmeorum.*
> *Io Dominus Umbrarum.*

[Perform the seasonal rite desired.]

[Perform any charms desired.]

Pass your hand over the drink, and say these or
similar words before taking a sip:

> *Old Ones, partake with me, and bless*
> *me on   the path.*

A More Ornate Sabbat Rite

This sabbat ritual is designed to celebrate the agricultural festivals of our ancestors. What follows is an outline ritual that can be supplemented with specific rites for each of the sabbats, all detailed in the pages following this ritual. The more ornate sabbat rite given here requires four candles, a cauldron or bowl of water, a besom, a dish of salt, incense, matches, a knife, a stang, an antlered skull, flora of the season, a cup of wine or beer, an offering bowl, a loaf of bread or cake, and any ingredients specific to the rite of the season.

Hold hand over the dish of salt.

> *I conjure thee, O creature of salt. Be thou pure and potent as the bones of the earth.*

Dip salt into water using knife.

I conjure thee, O creature of water. Be thou pure and potent as the roiling sea.

Light candle.

I conjure thee, O creature of fire. Be thou pure and potent as living flame.

Light the incense.

I conjure thee, O creature of incense. Be thou pure and potent as the voice ethereal.

Dip the besom in salt water, then asperge about the space in a circle.

I cleanse and purify this space with earth and water, that it be fit for the workings of my craft.

Carry incense about the room, fanning to disperse.

I cleanse and purify this space with fire and air, that it be fit for the workings of my craft.

Take up the stang, and drag around in a circle to demarcate the ring (widdershins, or counterclockwise, for dark work; deosil, or clockwise, for light work).

> *I conjure thee, O ring of art,*
> *by the North, East, South, and West.*
> *Be thou fit for the Old Ones, and be thou*
> *an emblem of the ancient alignment*
> *of those above and those below.*

Light the three candles beside the horned skull and flora upon the altar to represent the Old Ones.

Beat upon the ground with stang in a steady, slow rhythm.

> *One, two, three, and four.*
> *The Old Ones knock upon the door.*
> *Welcome them from floor to roof.*
> *Drink to them in a horse's hoof.*
> *Call the cat, the toad, the bran.*
> *Come to the feast, all ye who can.*
> *One, two, three, and four.*
> *The Old Ones are here, so no more.*

[Perform the rite specific to the sabbat at hand. See next section.]

[Perform any charms or magical work.]

Pass the knife horizontally over the cup of wine in a slicing motion.

Io regina pigmeorum.

Take a sip of the wine, and pour a portion into the offering bowl.

Cut a piece of the loaf with the knife.

Io dominus umbrarum.

Take a bite of the loaf, and place a portion into the offering bowl.

Spirits of the land, of the sea, of the sky,
spirits of the green earth,
spirits of the beasts,
Old Ones, draw us ever near
as we close the circle here.

All Hallow's Eve Rite

October 31st

This rite requires a smaller cauldron or pot and spool of twine or yarn. Toss the spool into the cauldron, and begin to slowly draw the twine from the cauldron.

> *Queen of Witches,*
> *Mother Nicneven*
> *who holds the clew,*
> *I call thy spirit unto me.*
> *Imbue this twine with your dark might,*
> *and be thou ever with me upon the path.*

Having drawn a sufficient length of twine, cut it loose, and wrap and tie it around the wrist. This twine can be kept for powerful ritual work or as a reminder of one's connection to the mother of witches.

The Twelfth Night
January 5th

This rite requires apple cider, a wooden cup or bowl, and an apple tree. (Note: if you don't have an apple tree on your property or room to plant one, consider visiting an orchard. Otherwise, if the climate is amenable, do think about planting an apple tree. The saplings are very affordable, and they are just lovely.)

Carry the cider out to the base of an apple tree.

> *Wassail, O wassail all over the mound.*
> *Our bread, it is white, and our ale,*
> *it is brown.*
> *Of polished wood is our wassail cup made.*
> *Wassail, O wassail, all over the glade.*

Pour the cider at the base of the tree.

The Candlemas Rite

February 2nd

This rite requires candles to be used throughout the year. Blessing them in advance amplifies their strength.

Take the central candle from the portion of the altar dedicated to the Old Ones. Begin to light all of the candles with its flame.

> *I will light the fire*
> *as Our Lady would light it.*
> *I cast her encirclement about this place*
> *and all present here.*
> *Blessed be the fire, the candles, and the house.*
> *Blessed be the people all*
> *on this eve, on this night,*
> *on each and every single night.*

The May Eve Rite
Last Night of April

This rite requires colored ribbons, which are to be tied decoratively on the branches of an old tree or shrub.

Tie the ribbons upon the tree or shrub, decorating it to honor the spirits of summer approaching.

> *Bless, O Old Ones,*
> *everything within my dwelling*
> *or in my possession,*
> *all loved ones, all creatures,*
> *all growing things,*
> *from May Eve to All Hallow's Eve,*
> *with goodly progress and gentle blessing,*
> *from sea to sea, and every river's mouth,*
> *from wave to wave, and to the base*
> *of the waterfall.*
> *When the kine forsake the stalls,*

when the sheep forsake the stalls,
when the goats ascend to the mount of mist,
may the tending of the Old Ones follow them.

The Midsummer Rite

June 21st

This rite requires the gathering of herbs for later use. Like the Candlemas rite, this working amplifies the power of ingredients to be used later in the year.

Take any herbs gathered or ready to be blessed for positive workings, and set them on the altar, pronouncing over them:

> *Hail be thou holy herb,*
> *plucked from the ground,*
> *friend unto the people,*
> *in love and kinship bound.*
> *Thou hast healed many a wound*
> *and soothed many a pain.*
> *Awaken now to keep thy word*
> *In Our Lady's name.*

Take any herbs gathered to be used for baneful

workings, and pronounce over them:

> *Hail be thou potent herb*
> *plucked from the ground,*
> *friend unto the poisoner,*
> *in wrath and vengeance bound.*
> *Thou hast ruined many a lord*
> *and inflicted many a pain.*
> *Awaken now to keep thy word*
> *in the Devil's name.*

The Lammas Rite

August 1st

This rite requires a round loaf of bread and a knife. Cut the loaf of bread into quarters. These will later be placed at the four corners of your home or property. Speak over them:

I conjure thee, O meal,
without which we could not live,
nourished by the light of the sun,
flowering amongst the fireflies,
who art kin unto the witches' line.
Be thou as the body of a great spirit
stretching to encompass us
from the four corners of this abode,
spirit unto body, body unto house,
house unto land, land unto Our Lady.

A Simple Esbat Rite

This ritual is designed to honor the full moon and requires only the simple altar composed of flora, fauna, and candle.

Take up the candle, light it, and walk around the space clockwise.

> *Here I set the ring about,*
> *Thout a thout and tout a tout.*

Set the candle upon the altar, and call to the Old Ones.

> *Io Regina Pigmeorum.*
> *Io Dominus Umbrarum.*

Turn your attention to the moon or to the direction where the moon would be.

> *Hail to thee, thou round moon,*

jewel of guidance in the night.
Hail to thee, thou round moon,
jewel of guidance on the billows.
Hail to thee, thou round moon,
jewel of guidance on the path.

[Perform any charms desired.]

Pass your hand over the drink, and say these or similar words before taking a sip:

Old Ones, partake with me, and bless
me on   the path.

A More Ornate Esbat Rite

This ritual is designed to honor the full moon and requires four candles, a cauldron or bowl of water, a besom, a dish of salt, incense, matches, a knife, a stang, an antlered skull, flora of the season, a cup of wine or beer, an offering bowl, and a loaf of bread or cake.

Hold hand over the dish of salt.

> *I conjure thee, O creature of salt. Be thou pure and potent as the bones of the earth.*

Dip salt into water using knife.

> *I conjure thee, O creature of water. Be thou pure and potent as the roiling sea.*

Light candle.

> *I conjure thee, O creature of fire. Be thou pure*

and potent as living flame.

Light the incense.

> *I conjure thee, O creature of incense. Be thou
> pure and potent as the voice ethereal.*

Dip the besom in salt water, then asperge about
the space in a circle.

> *I cleanse and purify this space with earth and
> water, that it be fit for the workings of my
> craft.*

Carry incense about the room, fanning to
disperse.

> *I cleanse and purify this space with fire and
> air, that it be fit for the workings of my craft.*

Take up the stang, and drag around in a circle
to demarcate the compass (widdershins, or
counterclockwise, for dark work; deosil, or
clockwise, for light work).

> *I conjure thee, O ring of art,*
> *by the North, East, South, and West.*
> *Be thou fit for the Old Ones, and be thou*
> *an emblem of the ancient alignment*

of those above and those below.

Light the three candles beside the horned skull and flora upon the altar to represent the Old Ones.

Beat upon the ground with stang in a steady, slow rhythm.

> *One, two, three, and four.*
> *The Old Ones knock upon the door.*
> *Welcome them from floor to roof.*
> *Drink to them in a horse's hoof.*
> *Call the cat, the toad, the bran.*
> *Come to the feast, all ye who can.*
> *One, two, three, and four.*
> *The Old Ones are here, so no more.*

Take the cauldron with salted water, and place it under the moon's light, reflecting the moon, if possible.

> *Hail to thee, thou round moon,*
> *jewel of guidance in the night.*
> *Hail to thee, thou round moon,*
> *jewel of guidance on the billows.*
> *Hail to thee, thou round moon,*
> *jewel of guidance on the ocean.*
> *Hail to thee, thou round moon,*

jewel of guidance on the path.
Hail to thee, thou round moon,
jewel of guidance of my heart.
I draw a portion of thy spirit
into this vessel of water.
May thy light be fair to me.
May thy course be smooth to me,
thou fair lamp of grace,
thou fair moon of the seasons.

Scry upon the water's reflection for revelations.

[Perform any charms or magical work.]

Pass the knife horizontally over the cup of wine in a slicing motion.

Io regina pigmeorum.

Take a sip of the wine, and pour a portion into the offering bowl.

Cut a piece of the loaf with the knife.

Io dominus umbrarum.

Take a bite of the loaf, and place a portion into the offering bowl.

Spirits of the land, of the sea, of the sky,
spirits of the green earth,
spirits of the beasts,
Old Ones, draw us ever near
as we close the circle here.

A Rite of Dedication

This rite does not require any ingredients and may be performed as often as one likes in order to reaffirm one's dedication to the path. It involves repeating the Lord's Prayer backwards. Witch-lore tells us that it is sometimes necessary to shake off the shackles of the dominant religion in order to make progress in the craft.

Alone and in a dark, candlelit room, repeat:

> *Nema livee, morf su revilled tub*
> *noishaytpmet ootni ton suh deel sus*
> *tshaiga sapsert taht yeth*
> *vigrawf eu za sesapsert rua*
> *suh vigrawf derb ilaid rua yed sith*
> *suh vig neveh ni si za thre ni nud*
> *eeb liw eyth muck modngik eyth*
> *main eyth eeb dwohlah nevah*
> *ni tra chioo, retharf rua.*

Place left hand under left foot and right hand over head.

> *Old Ones, all that is between my hands*
> *is of thee and the ways.*
>
> *Io regina pigmeorum.*
> *Io dominus umbrarum.*

Conjuration of Nicneven

This incantation sometimes entails dancing or walking in a circle around a fire in order to conjure the Scottish witch-queen. It is sometimes referred to as the "witches' reel." The word "commer" is a term to describe a companion or friend, usually female.

Commer, go ye before!
Commer, go ye!
If ye will not go before,
Commer, let me!
Ring-a-ring a widdershins,
a whirlin' skirlin' widdershins!
Commer, Carlin, Crone, and Queen!
Three times three!

Conjuration of the King of Elphame

This conjuration has its source in an old ballad. It describes a marriage between the human and spirit world, contingent upon the performance of impossible tasks. In witch-lore, the King of Elphame is often another form of the Devil.

> There stand three trumpeters on the hill.
> Blow, blow, blow, winds, blow.
> They blow their pipes so loud and shrill,
> and the wind shall blow thy spirit nigh.
>
> I'll knit thee a finest linen shirt-
> blow, blow, blow, winds, blow-
> without one stitch of needlework,
> and the wind shall blow thy spirit nigh.
>
> I'll hang the shirt upon a thorn-

blow, blow, blow, winds, blow-
that by no son of man was sown,
and the wind shall blow thy spirit nigh.

The thorn be watered from a well-
blow, blow, blow, winds, blow-
that never a drop or trickle filled,
and the wind shall blow thy spirit nigh.

Conjuration of Aradia

The spirit of Aradia is described in Leland's work as the daughter of Diana and her brother Lucifer. She is the called "the first of witches known." Part of the Aradia lore is her promise to answer the calls of witches in the future with her aid. This charm should be performed with water, wine, and a bag of salt.

> *Thus do I seek Aradia, Aradia, Aradia!*
> *At midnight, I bless myself*
> *with water, wine, and a bag of salt.*
> *I bless myself with water, wine, and salt*
> *to implore a favor from Aradia.*
>
> *Aradia, my Aradia,*
> *daughter of Lucifer and Diana,*
> *whose mother did repent her fault*
> *and fashion thee a spirit benevolent!*
>
> *Aradia! Aradia!*

I implore thee by the love
thy mother had for thee
and by the love which I, too, feel for thee!
Aradia, grant the grace I ask of thee.

Conjuration of the Folletino Rosso

Another entity described in Leland's work, the Folletino Rosso (translated loosely as "Red Goblin") is a familiar spirit associated with round stones.

> *Spirit of good omen, come to my aid.*
> *Spirit of the Folletino Rosso,*
> *abandon me not.*
>
> *Enter now this round stone*
> *that in my pocket I may carry thee*
> *to call unto thee when I have need of thee.*
> *Abandon me not by day or night.*
>
> *Folletino Rosso, collect my debts*
> *from those who would withhold from me.*
> *Folletino Rosso, frighten my enemies*
> *who seek to plot against me.*

Folletino Rosso, keep close my loved ones.
Folletino Rosso, bring me favor and luck.
Folletino Rosso, come thou to my aid.

Accompany me in thy dwelling of round stone
and abandon me not by night or day.

Conjuration of the Wag at the Wa'

This charm involves a crook or cast iron instrument used to hang pots over an old kitchen-fire. A horseshoe or other hanging object with an upward-facing swoop will do. It is swung back and forth over a flame while reciting the charm. (This spirit enjoys perching in the curve of metal objects, so be sure the curve faces up to make a proper seat when it is hung in the house.)

> *Wag-at-the-wa' went out in the night*
> *to see that the moon was shining bright.*
> *The moon, she was at the latter fa'.*
> *Come, by and by, O Wag-at-the-wa'.*
>
> *Why do you wag the witch's nicket-crook*
> *when the pyet's asleep where the corbies rook?*

Come thou in from the wind and cold
to the warm perch that I now hold.

Conjuration of the Hobbitrot

This spirit is fond of spinning and sewing and is associated with the holed stone, which should be used to summon her.

You who live in the dreary den
are both fair and foul to see,
hidden from the glorious sun
that seems all fair earth's canopie.

Ever must thine evenings lone
be spent on the colladie-stone,
cheerless as the evening grey,
when Causlem dies, the moon away.

Come, now blithe and ever fair,
to breathe the dark, chill evening air
and lean upon the self-bored stone,
unseen to all but I alone.

Conjuration of the Black Book of the Art

This incantation, sourced in *Folger Shakespeare Library MS. V.b.26*, is provided with little guidance in its original description, but has proven useful for shifting consciousness and accessing the hidden knowledge of magical currents. The initiatory spirit associated with the teaching and guidance of student witches in the old lore is sometimes called "the Man of the Sabbat," who offers access to the black book of the art, which is the source of all magical knowledge.

> *Obymero, per noctem*
> *et symeam*
> *et membres membris*
> *et larys cawtis*
> *nomis et arypys.*

A Song of Flight to the Sabbat

This charm is taken from two sources. The first is an old ballad that can be found in remote parts of North America and the British isles. The second is an incantation provided by Scottish witch, Isabel Gowdie. In the lore, witches use charms such as these with a stick, stang, or the long stalk of a weed in order to travel via spirit flight.

> *I call a gray horse. I call a gray mare.*
> *Gray mane, gray tail,*
> *gray stripe down her back,*
> *and not a hair on her that isn't coal black.*
>
> *Come king, come queen,*
> *come company more,*
> *all riding behind and walking before.*
>
> *Come stark-naked drummer,*
> *a-beating your drum,*

By stang and by beast, come a-marching along.

Horse and hattock! Horse and go!
Horse and pellatis! Ho! Ho!

Another Song of Sabbat-Flight

This incantation is derived from a medieval play, but it is thoroughly rooted in the themes of witch-lore. The text describes conjuring the Devil as well as flight and other magical acts pertaining to the sabbat.

Bazabi lacha bachabe!
Lamac cahi achababe!
Karrellyos!
Lamac lamec Bachalyos!
Cabahagy Sabalyos!
Baryolos!
Lagaz atha Cabyolas!
Samahac atha Famolas!
Hurrahya!

Songs for Going forth as Beasts

This incantation describes the transmogrification of the witch into various animal forms. The verses are useful as rhythmic chants and are accompanied by the use of techniques of spirit flight in animal form described in the second section of this book. "Meckle" is another way of saying "much."

And I shall go into a hare
with sorrow and sighing and meckle care,
and I shall go in the Devil's name
until I come home again.

And I shall go into a crow
with sorrow and sighing and blackest throw,
and I shall go in the Devil's name
until I come home again.

And I shall go into a cat
with sorrow and sighing and a black shot,

and I shall go in the Devil's name
until I come home again.

And I shall go into a goat
with blackest hooves and blackest coat,
and I shall go in the Devil's name
until I come home again.

Into the shape of a ____ I go
with blackest shot and blackest throw,
and I shall go in the Devil's name
until I come home again.

The White Paternoster

The White Paternoster is one of three charms described in the witch-lore. It is derived from the introduction of latin charms by the church among largely illiterate pagan folk in Scotland, who adapted the incantations for use in a variety of circumstances. The White Paternoster was used for blessing and protecting. My own version is as follows:

White Paternoster, stronger and faster
than harm by foe and all disaster,
come trumpet and soldier,
come mistress and master,
as I now speak the White Paternoster.

Pater noster qui es in coelis,
sanctificetur nomen tuum;
adveniat regnum tuum,
fiat voluntas tua
sicut tu coelo et tu terra.

Panem nostrum quotidianum
da nobis hodie,
et dimitte nobis debita nostra.
Sicut et nos dimittimus debitoribus nostris.
Et ne nosindueas in temtationem
sed libera nos a malo.

The Black Paternoster

One of the three Paternosters, this charm can be found in an multitude of forms in folkloric volumes. It is sometimes associated with defense against death, disease, and other ills. Another popular version of this charm is well-known to many English language-speakers as a bedtime prayer addressing the "four corners of my bed." The form here includes a backwards version of the White Paternoster.

Come thou, corners of earth, sea, and sky
to protect and guide me in darkness.
Olam a son arabil des
menoitatnet ni sacudnison en te
sortson subirotibed sumittimid son te tucis,
artson atibed sibon ettimid te,
eidoh sibon ad
muraiditouq murtson menap.

Old Ones, be thou before me,
behind me, on my right and my left,
above and below me as a shield in the night.
Arret ni te oleoc ni tucis
aut satnulov taif,
muut munger tainevda;

muut nemon rutecifitcaas,
sileoc mi se iuq retson retap.

The Green Paternoster

This charm is adapted from several incantations related to the third and most unique of the Paternosters. The Green Paternoster specifically addresses Bride as Mary's midwife. My own version is as follows:

Green Paternoster,
Mary's sweet sister,
who knew every charm
of midwife and healer,
be thou my guardian,
be thou my foster
as long as I say
the Green Paternoster.

A Charm for Removal

Among the many known charms for removing illness, reducing fever, banishing baneful spirits, and removing unwelcome influences, the following written and spoken charm appears in many grimoires and folk magical texts. This incantation is written on a piece of parchment that is placed on the patient, each line dissolving slowly until it is no more.

ABAXACATABAX
ABAXACATABA
ABAXACATAB
ABAXACATA
ABAXACAT
ABAXACA
ABAXAC
ABAXA
ABAX
ABA
AB
A

The Poppet

Perhaps one of the most infamous tools of old-style witchery, the poppet can be fashioned from wheat, corn husks, fabric, clay, or wax, and is designed to form a sympathetic link with the target.

Fashion a doll in the likeness of the target. This image can be made from anything, so long as it is hand made. A simple process uses soaked corn husks, tied and manipulated in a series of steps depicted on the next page. Add to it such details and engravings to indicate that it is connected to the person deeply. Chant over it:

Ailif, casyl, zaze,
hit mel meltat.

Any actions performed to the poppet will take a similar effect on the target. Likewise, setting the poppet in a container with other objects will bring the represented influences into the target's life via sympathetica (examples: roses for love, nettles for suffering, snakeskin for enemies, seashells for protection).

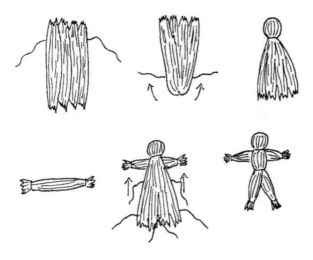

The Nine Herbs Charm

Traditionally, this Saxon charm is spoken over a salve prepared from the nine herbs, which is applied to the target's body. The witch then blows into the target's ears and mouth to remove the harmful spirit.

Remember, Mugwort, what you revealed, what you made known on the great proclamation. You were called Oria, oldest of herbs, and you have power against three and against thirty. You have power against poison and against infection. You have power against the loathsome foe running through the land.

And you, Plantain, mother of herbs, open from the East, mighty within. Over you, chariots creaked. Over you, queens rode. Over you, brides cried out. Over you, bulls snorted. You withstood them all. You dashed against them. May you likewise withstand poison and infection and the loathsome foe running through the land.

Remember herb, that Stune is your name. You grow on a stone. You stand up against poison. You dash against poison. You drive out the hostile one. You cast out poison.

Nettle are you called. You attack against poison. You are the herb that fought against the serpent. You have power against poison and infection. You have power against the loathsome foe roaming through the land.

Remember, Chamomile, what you made known, what you accomplished at Alorford, that man should never lose his life from infection once chamomile is prepared for his food.

Remember, herb, that you are called Wergulu. A seal sent you across the sea, a vexation against poison, a help to many. You stand against pains. You dash against poison.

A worm came crawling, and it killed nothing.

For Woden took nine glory-twigs; he smote the adder so that it flew apart into nine parts.

There, Apple, you succeeded against the poison, that serpents may never dwell in the house.

Chervil and Fennel, you two of such might, you were

created by the wise lord, holy in heaven as he hung. He set and sent you to the seven worlds, to the wretched and the fortunate, as a help to all in need.

You stand against poison. You fight against poison. You avail against three and against thirty, against the hand of the foe and against the noble scheming, against all of the enchantmenes of vile creatures.

Now, these nine herbs have power against nine evil spirits, against nine poisons and against nine infections: against the red poison, against the foul poison, against the white poison, against the pale blue poison, against the black poison, against the blue poison, against the brown poison, against the crimson poison.

Against worm blister, against water blister, against thorn blister, against thistle blister, against ice blister, against poison blister.

Against any poison come from the East or the North or the South or the West among the people.

I alone know a running stream, and the nine adders beware of it. May all the weeds spring up from their roots, the seas slip apart, all salt water, when I blow this poison from you.

To Bless or Curse by Gesture

Pointing or touching with one of the fingers has long been associated with blessing and cursing. In Scottish witchcraft, a simple curse is performed by pointing with the index finger, while a simple blessing performed with the thumb, during which the witch speaks a version of the charm, such as the following:

> *Ill may thee thrive, and ill may thee stead.*
> *The sticks of hell light on thee,*
> *and hell's cauldron mayest thou seeth therein,*
> *thy bones to rake about the stygian banks.*
> *In the Devil's name, I pray it.*

Or, alternatively:

> *Well may thee thrive,*
> *and well may thee stead.*
> *Blessed waters refresh thee,*
> *and the cup of life mayest thou drink thereof,*

thy blood protected from shore to shore.
In Our Lady's name, I pray it.

The Charmed Sachet

Magical herbs may be packed into a small talisman called a "sachet," which is made of sewn cloth. These charms can be made in a variety of colors and decorated with sigils stitched into the fabric. Often, the witch will include a more complex incantation or statement of intent on a piece of paper, which is folded and sewn inside along with the herbs.

Charm of the Firefly

This charm can be used for augury by studying the movement of a firefly caught in a glass, but it can also be used for wish fulfillment by whispering the desire to the firefly and releasing it.

Queen of the fireflies,
hurry apace.
Come to me now
as if running a race.
Come to me now
as you hear my voice sing.
Bridle, O bridle
the son of the king.

A Counter-charm

To return baneful magic unto the sender, form the hand into the gesture of the horns (index and pinkie fingers out), facing the enemy or a representation thereof, and speak the charm:

Contrere brachia iniqui rei
et lingua maligna subvertetur.

To Drive Malicious Spirits from the Home

Place in the four corners of the home a piece of parchment on which you have written the following charm. This may also be spoken in the four corners of the home while fumigating with incense.

Omnis spiritus laudet dominum:
mosen habert et prophetas:
exurgat deus et dissipentur inimici ejus.

The Curse of the Evil Eye

To fashion the eye, gather a piece of wood, and inscribe upon it the image of an eye. Surround it with the names of your familiars who will carry out your vengeance. In the center of the eye, write the name of the target. While driving a nail through the center of the eye, speak the charm:

Justa judicia tua!

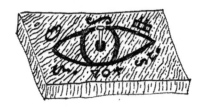

To Speak with the Dead

Conversing with the dead is sometimes referred to as necromancy. This charm, derived from the 15th century, is designed to be used with the same techniques for perceiving spirits described earlier in this book. In a plot of bare soil, lay a tablet on which the following charm is written:

t B R I P a R
I C I P A S S
E Z P L a T M
E X W I a M E
Q E W a R E N
P R I E Z T

A Braided Charm

This particular incantation is sourced in the work of William Shakespeare. Take three strands of twine, yarn, or string while focusing on your need. While braiding, speak the charm:

> *Weird sisters, hand in hand,*
> *posters over sea and land,*
> *thus do go about, about.*
> *Thrice to thine,*
> *and thrice to mine,*
> *and thrice again to make up nine.*

When the cord is of a good length to wear as a bracelet or necklace, say:

> *Peace. The charm's wound up.*

To Protect against Maleficium and Wicked Spirits

This charm of defense and blessing was used against "elf-shot," a kind of attack from the spirit world that could be performed by faeries or by witches during spirit-flight.

I charge thee against arrowshot,
against doorshot, against wombshot,
against eyeshot, against tongueshot,
against livershot, against lungshot
against heartshot, all the most.
In our Lady's name, I pray it.

The Witches' Ladder

One of the most widely known charms
for accomplishing a variety of objectives (based
on whatever the desired outcome may be) is the
witches' ladder. This is a length of yarn or
twine into which nine feathers have been
knotted. As each knot is tied, the witch speaks
the appropriate charm. For example:

I tie this knot for my need of ____.
The next I tie in the Devil's name.
The third to fix it by my will.
The fourth one to hold it fast and firm.
The fifth one to bind it evermore.
The sixth fastens the wish herein.
The seventh brings it nearer still.
The eighth makes it almost true.
The ninth completes the ladder by which
I climb and reach for ____.

Talismans

Although many image-based charms can be derived from personal revelations via familiar spirits, the images on the following page represent a selection from Folger Shakespeare Library MS. V.b.26. The first is designed to bring attraction and love. The second wins friends and favor. The third compels malevolent spirits to restrain themselves from harming the practitioner. The final seven represent the planetary forces of Saturn (a), Jupiter (b), Mars (c), the Sun (d), Venus (e), Mercury (f), and the Moon (g).

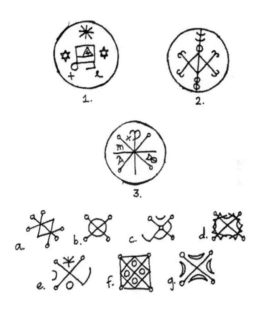

1.

2.

3.

a. b. c. d.

e. f. g.

223

A Lustration Charm

Water's cleansing properties lend it naturally to charms for blessing afflicted persons and removing unwanted influences. This rite, adapted from the *Carmina Gadelica*, is meant to be recited while cupping water and pouring "palmfuls" over the intended person's head.

> *A palmful for thine age,*
> *a palmful for thy growth,*
> *a palmful for thy throat,*
> *a flood for thine appetite.*
>
> *For thy share of the bounty,*
> *crowdie and kail;*
> *For thy share of the taking,*
> *honey and warm milk.*
>
> *For thy share of the supping,*
> *whisked whey and fat;*

For thy share of the spoil,
with bow and with spear.

For thy share of the preparation,
the yellow eggs of Easter;
For thy share of the treat,
my treasure and my joy.

For thy share of the feast
with gifts and with tribute;
For thy share of the treasure,
pulset of my love.

For thy share of the chase
up the face of Beinn-a-cheo;
For thy share of the hunting
and the ruling over hosts.

For thy share of palaces
and the courts of kings;

For thy share of paradise
with its goodness and its peace.

The part of thee that does not grow at dawn,
may it grow at eventide;

The part of thee that does not grow at night,
may it grow at ridge of middle-day.

*Three palmfuls to preserve thee
from every envy, evil eye, and death:
three palmfuls of the sacred waters
of life, of love, and of peace.*

Rowan and Red Thread

This simple talisman is made of rowan berries, pierced and dried, then strung on a red thread. Over it, the following charm is spoken to awaken its protective qualities:

Rowan berry and red thread,
bring all evil to its sped.

A Charm for Prosperity

Take three buttercup or similar yellow flowers, and set them into a bag or charm bottle, one at a time, while speaking:

Three ladies roamed across the land,
each with a piece of gold in her hand.

The first one said, "I want some."

The second one said, "I need some."

The third one said, "I have some, just as I
wished: plenty of gold to fill my dish."

An Abjuration of the Spirit

This abjuration, adapted from the Greek Magical Papyri, calls on Hecate in her aspect as as the Lady of Tartarus or Queen of the Underworld. It should only be employed when a spirit greatly offends and no further contact is desired.

> *I am an initiate of Hekate Ereschkigal,*
> *Hekate Propolos,*
> *Hekate Phosphoros,*
> *Hekate Chthonia,*
> *Hekate Trimorphos,*
> *Hekate, Lady of Tartarus,*
> *Hekate, undefeatable,*
> *Hekate, in whose great darkness*
> *your small shadow is dissolved as nothing,*
> *and in whose name I abjure thee*
> *and all signs and forms of thee.*

Notes on Herbs

Foxglove is associated with both faeries and witches. In the lore, witches wear its flowers as thimbles. It is a deadly plant from which many modern heart medicines are derived. It controls the pulse and flow of blood (for good or ill), and so it is an herb connected to both life and death and the passages in-between.

Milk Thistle can be boiled to call spirits. It can also be worn for protection, vitality, and virility. Legend tells that the an invading army was defeated once because one of their number stepped on a thistle and screamed, alerting nearby warriors.

Lemon balm is associated with Venus for its sweet scent, but its lemony flavor also imbues it with lunar properties. It is useful in dream work and spirit flight, and its powers are soothing and calming.

Plantain is associated with resilience, strength, and the ability to outlast enemies and obstacles due to its ability to thrive on roadsides and spring back after being trampled.

Deadnettle can be worn as a talisman against depression. It is associated with the ability to thrive in the face of dark times and crises. It is a kind protector and resists darkness.

Horsenettle is a dangerous poison, though not as potent as other members of the nightshade family. It is prepared as a tincture for cursing objects. It should never be ingested, and it should be handled with gloves due to its sharp thorns.

Chicory can be infused into oil and applied to the body to find favor from those in power and for success in business dealings. It is also associated with removing obstacles and can be used as a talisman.

Violet is associated with the beloved dead and the banishment of evil spirits. Its leaves can be used as talismans to bring love.

Buttercup's bright and cheerful nature lends it to

use restoring innocence and joy. It is also associated with prosperity and abundance due to its butter-like coloration.

Chickweed has a very lunar nature due to its ability to hold moisture and thrive in the cold. It is associated with protection and resilience, and it is employed in charms of fidelity and to ensure a deep and lasting love between two people.

Lady's thumb can be prepared in a sachet to bind a lover to you. Its stalks have a webbed "binding" that resemble a sleeve being pulled away from a thumb. Its flowers area lovely and delicate.

Mallow is often prepared as an unguent and applied to the body in order to protect against harm and cushion the wearer from metaphorical "barbs" he or she may encounter.

Notes on Colors

Red is associated with life-blood and resiliencce. It is the color of life and of ripe fruit, berries, and flowers. It brings protection from the powers of death and vibrance in the face of adversity.

White is the color of purity. Its associations include cleansing, clarity, and beginnings. Like snow that falls early in the year, it precedes new growth with its blank slate.

Black is associated with darkness and with strength. Because black cannot be stained, but instead absorbs adversity, this color brings powerful defense. Like the raven, it is also associated with death, with those who dwell beneath the land, and with doorways to the unknown.

Gray is a color of vastness and wild energy. Like

the sea and the stormy skies, gray is dangerous, tempestuous, and energetic. It is associated with the wild hunt and with spirits who ride about on the winds. This color pertains to permutations and change.

Green is a faerie color and is associated with land spirits, with dreams, and with thriving flora. It is also a color of cunning and trickery. Green fascinates with its beauty, but in doing so, it can either help or hurt.

Yellow, the color of butter, honey, grains, and gold, represents wealth and fecundity. Its presence communicates riches either material or spiritual. It is associated with possessions, fertility, and prosperity.

Blue is associated with memory, the beloved dead and ancestors, and the lifting of curses and depression. It is a color associated with especially good fortune since it is more complicated to produce as a dye.

The best all-purpose colors for candles, sachets, and talismans is undyed natural fiber: usually tan, cream, or beige. Most of our ancestors' tools were undyed.

Notes on Magical Timing

Lunar phases govern the magic of increase (waxing) and decrease (waning). The dark moon is appropriate for foresight and divination. The full moon is suitable for all works of magic.

The days of the week lend themselves to planetery forces. Sunday, ruled by the Sun, is suitable for works of joy and prosperity. Monday, ruled by the moon, governs dreams and intuition. Tuesday, under the influence of Mars, is ideal for conflict, victory, and control over enemies. Wednesday is of Mercury, and it is well-suited for works of travel, communication, and commerce. Thursday, ruled by Jupiter, can empower charms seeking favor from those in power or in legal or financial matters. Friday, favored by Venus, is suitable for love and attraction magic. Saturday, ruled by Saturn, is ideal for cursing and necromancy.

The tides of the year also influence magical currents. The weeks from All Hallow's Eve to Candlemas represent the resting tide, ideal for recovery and communion with those who have gone before. From Candlemas to May Eve falls the cleansing tide, suited to clearing away that which is no longer needed. From May Eve to Lammas comes the growing tide, ideal for all magic related to increases. The weeks from Lammas to All Hallow's Eve mark the reaping tide, a period connected to gathering one's dues and calling in favors.

Notes on Cartomancy

There are many modern systems of cartomancy, and many more methods unique to the practitioner. The diversity of approaches to reading playing cards is evidenced in the plethora of chapbooks and manuals published in the 1800s and early 1900s detailing diverse interpretations of the cards. Usually, the numbers and suits are cross-analyzed to form some meaning specific to each individual card, which are interpreted by their position in the spread.

The simplest form of this process interprets the suits as pertaining to love and relationships (hearts), work and projects (spades), passion and creativity (clubs), and possessions and assets (diamonds). The numbers are read as pertaining to beginnings (1s), relationships and exchanges (2s), growth or increase (3s), stability (4s), chaos or wild energy (5s), harmony and balance (6s), vanity and self-care (7s), movement and intellect (8s), attainment or achievement (9s), and endings (10s). Jacks, queens, and kings are read as zodiacal aspects of the querent's personality. Jacks represent mutable signs, while queens are mutable and kings are fixed. The suits are read as elements, with diamonds corresponding to earth, clubs to fire, hearts to water, and spades to air.

Thus, the king of spades is interpreted as the aquarian aspect of the querent's personality, the fixed sign of air, marked by ingenuity and inquisitiveness. The four of diamonds is interpreted as the stability of income or resources at the querent's disposal. The ten of hearts may mark the end of a relationship of some kind.

A tried and true spread from my own practice relies on only eight cards: two rows of three, and above them, one card set upon the other horizontally, forming a cross. I call it "the churchyard spread" because of its likeness to a church or a headstone. The two rows of three are read as movements from left to right; the card to the left represents the force that is leaving the querent's life and needs to be released, and the card on the right represents that which is arriving and should be embraced. The card in the center represents the current

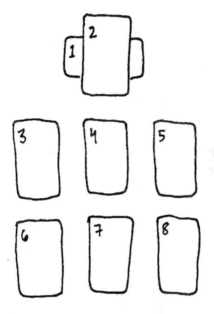

tool at the querent's disposal. Together, these form two "advisory lines" of recommended action at this time. The two cards crossed above represent the querent (the bottom card) and the opportunity for learning or growth that is currently presenting itself in the querent's life (the top card).

Thus, if cards 1 and 2 are the eight of diamonds and the queen of hearts, this may represent a person of learning or achievement who is currently feeling pulled towards dreams and artistic endeavors (Piscean influence).

If the first advisory line is composed of the three of clubs, the jack of spades, and the nine of diamonds, the querent is being advised to release opportunities to increase workload while embracing rewards and achievements from recent effort. Since the jack of spades represents the mutable powers of air and the sign of libra, the querent is currently empowered with many libra qualities, such as charm, kindness, and an ability to bring things into greater balance.

Magical Alphabets

The use of the Theban alphabet as well as other magical alphabets may be incorporated in the fashioning of talismans, fetishes, spirit bottles, sachets, and other items for magical use. The Theban alphabet is of uncertain origins, but has a long history of use in magic, appearing in many grimoires and magical manuals from as early as the 1500s.

A Witches' Rann

Well do I know my name and path,
and well do I keep familiar craft.
Thirteen full moons grace the year;
at each, summon the Old Ones near.
Six times mark the season's ring;
at each of these, make offering.
Let the ring be drawn around
to welcome those beneath the mound.
Seek the dreaming sabbat-glade
where craft is wrought and pacts are made.
Let the charms be gleaned from lore
where elders worked their craft before,
but let the rites be made anew
as branches from the trunk are hewn.
The sacred knowledge of the art
is kept in neither vial nor chart.
Seek wisdom in the growing things,
in serpent skin and owlet wing,
in the spinning of the wheel,
altars at which all things must kneel.

Seek to hear and understand
the familiar spirit's speech and hand.
None may train or test or teach
as the shadow given each.
Ever seek the One Black Book
in which no living thing may look.

Conclusion: Whither the Modern Folk Witch?

In our fast-paced, tech-savvy, commercial world, it is sometimes difficult to find things of lasting value. We have, in many ways, created a world in which it is more feasible to purchase a thing than to make it with our hands, easier to sell our time (which is to say, portions of our lives) than to survive on our own creativity and the sweat off our brows. This is not to say that modernity hasn't solved many important problems (antibiotics, public education, and libraries, anyone?), but we can't ignore its more insidious conditions.

This sacrifice of simplicity for convenience affects our spiritual lives as well. It is easy to buy a book, even ten books, that promise to teach the complete secrets of yoga, of the tarot, and yes, even of witchcraft. Ingredients and dried herbs imported from all over the planet can be had at the click of a button. Stones mined from impoverished countries are cheap to order. The commodification of mystery cheapens our practices our magics -- like a faint scent of plastic that can't be washed from a sweater made in a factory. Our hunger for something earnest and true sends us reeling and makes us angry. Meanwhile, we poison our bodies, our planet, and our magics.

By returning to the careful study of the lore, closeness with the land, and communion with our familiar spirits, we undergo an initiation both old and new: old because it connects us with the lore of previous generations, and new because we encounter first-hand the initiating spirits of folk witchcraft. In *learning to learn* witchcraft through these earnest initiatory currents, we sever ourselves from the machinery of new age commodification and form a personalized, firmly rooted craft practice that is both ancient and modern.

In seeking authentic spiritual practices, some modern pagans have veered into unfortunate patterns. Some modern groups have sought to glorify ethnic lineage, as if genetics has anything to do with one's ability to access the spirit world. In the United States, some traditions with mostly white members have appropriated African American and Latin American magical practices and rebranded them as a kind of "rootsy" witchcraft in a spiritual form of white-washing. Others have ritualized sex acts to such a degree that new initiates feel pressured to participate in unsavory rituals in order to grow in the craft. A vast majority of modern witchcraft groups are influenced by gender essentialist assumptions about "maleness" and "femaleness," worshipping simplistic gender roles as a kind of "divine polarity" that leaves queer folks (and, indeed, anyone who doesn't fit the heteronormative mold) outside of the circle.

If we look closely to the witch-lore, we find a world that is diverse, complex, and pluralistic. There are very few rules and paradigms in old craft. In fact, because the bodies of lore we have inherited come from many individuals working in many cultures, there is often paradox. In one culture, the serpent may hold very different connotations than another. It is part of the folk witch's journey to identify and refine the focus of her craft over time and interpret it through a modern lens. This discernment, conducted under the guidance of familiar spirits, includes thinking carefully about the modern implications of the racist, sexist, and homophobic baggage we have inherited.

I believe that the spirit of witchcraft, at its heart, speaks to a kind of freedom that some of us are called to, even if we try to shirk off the pull towards strange, dark paths. Our power comes from strength of will, and our flight is the untethered, limitless dream we conjure. The Old Ones, I believe, are with us: whispering around a candle lit in a dark room, reaching for us beyond a line of trees in the moonlight. I believe that the old spirits are alive and well, even if they are sometimes hidden from our sight, obfuscated by what we want or choose to see instead, by our inability to accept our freedom and innate access to deep wisdom.

For the modern folk witch, the primary barrier to the sabbat-grove lies in ourselves. Can we call to the familiar spirit still? Can we pluck a cure from the cold ground? Can we discern wisdom in the movement of a candle's flame, in the laying of a pack of cards? Can we accept the old lore as our teacher and our guide? Can we hear the voice of the wind? Can we listen to a weed? Can we fly?

Bibliography and Further Reading

Campbell, John Gregorson. *Superstitions of the Highlands and Islands of Scotland,* Glasgow, J. MacLehose, 1900.

Campbell, John Gregorson. *Witchcraft and the Second Sight in the Highlands and Islands of Scotland,* Glasgow, J. MacLehose, 1902.

Carmichael, Alexander. *Carmina Gadelica,* Edinburgh, MacLeod, 1900.

Chumbley, Andrew. *Opuscula Magica,* vol. 1, 2, and 3, California, Three Hands Press, 2011.

Cochrane, Robert. *The Robert Cochrane Letters,* Somerset, Capall Bann, 2002.

Culpeper, Nicholas. *The Complete Herbal,* London, Thomas Kelly, 1653.

Dalyell, John Graham. *The Darker Superstitions of Scotland,* Edinburgh, Waugh and Inns, 1834.

Folkard, Richard. *Plant Lore, Legends, and Lyrics: Embracing the Myths, Traditions, Superstitions, and Folk-lore of the Plant Kingdom,* London, S. Low, Marston, Searle, and Rivington, 1884.

Frazer, James George. *The Golden Bough: A Study in Magic and Religion,* London,

Macmillan, 1890.

Guazzo, Francesco Maria. *Compendium Maleficarum*. Milan, Italy, Apud Haeredes, 1608.

Harms, Daniel, James R. Clark, and Joseph H. Peterson. *The Book of Oberon: A Sourcebook of Elizabethan Magic,* Minnesota, Llewellyn Publications, 2015.

Hohman, Johann Georg. *The Long Lost Friend,* Harrisburg, PA, 1850.

Howard, Michael. *Witches and Wizards of Scotland,* California, Three Hands Press, 2013.

Kirk, Robert. *The Secret Commonwealth of Elves, Fauns, and Fairies,* London, Nutt, 1893.

Leland, Charles G. *Aradia, or, Gospel of the Witches (of Italy),* London, 1899.

Murray, Margaret Alice. *The Witch-Cult in Western Europe,* Oxford, Clarendon Press, 1921.

Thompson, R. Lowe. *The History of the Devil: Horned God of the West,* London, Kegan, Paul, Trench, Trubner & Co., 1929.

Scot, Reginald. *The Discoverie of Witchcraft,* London, Richard Cotes, 1584.

Sluijs, Marinus Anthony. *Traditional Cosmology,* vol. 3, London, All-Around Publications, 2011.

Spare, Austin Osman. *The Book of Pleasure: The*

Psychology of Ecstasy, London, Spare, 1913.

Thiselton-Dyer, T. F. *The Mythic and Magickal Folklore of Plants,* Samhain Song Press, 2008.

Trevelyan, Marie. *Folk-lore and Folk-stories of Wales,* London, E. Stock, 1909.

Trithemius, Johanne. *Polygraphia,* Germany, 1815.

Weyer, Johann. "Pseudomonarchia Daemonum, "in *De Praestigiis Daemonum,* Basileae Oporinianus, 1568.

Wilkie, Thomas. "Old Rites, Ceremonies, and Customs of the Southern Counties of Scotland." In *The History of the Berwickshire Naturalists' Club,* vol. 23, 1916.

Made in the USA
Monee, IL
20 June 2024

60180326R10150